There Is No Need to Talk about This

TRANSGRESSIONS: CULTURAL STUDIES AND EDUCATION

Series Editor:
Shirley R. Steinberg, *University of Calgary, Canada*

Founding Editor:
Joe L. Kincheloe (1950-2008) *The Paulo and Nita Freire International Project for Critical Pedagogy*

Editorial Board

Rochelle Brock, *Indiana University Northwest, USA*
Rhonda Hammer, *UCLA, USA*
Luis Huerta-Charles, *New Mexico State University, USA*
Christine Quail, *McMaster University, Canada*
Jackie Seidel, *University of Calgary, Canada*
Mark Vicars, *Victoria University, Queensland, Australia*

This book series is dedicated to the radical love and actions of Paulo Freire, Jesus "Pato" Gomez, and Joe L. Kincheloe.

TRANSGRESSIONS: CULTURAL STUDIES AND EDUCATION

Cultural studies provides an analytical toolbox for both making sense of educational practice and extending the insights of educational professionals into their labors. In this context *Transgressions: Cultural Studies and Education* provides a collection of books in the domain that specify this assertion. Crafted for an audience of teachers, teacher educators, scholars and students of cultural studies and others interested in cultural studies and pedagogy, the series documents both the possibilities of and the controversies surrounding the intersection of cultural studies and education. The editors and the authors of this series do not assume that the interaction of cultural studies and education devalues other types of knowledge and analytical forms. Rather the intersection of these knowledge disciplines offers a rejuvenating, optimistic, and positive perspective on education and educational institutions. Some might describe its contribution as democratic, emancipatory, and transformative. The editors and authors maintain that cultural studies helps free educators from sterile, monolithic analyses that have for too long undermined efforts to think of educational practices by providing other words, new languages, and fresh metaphors. Operating in an interdisciplinary cosmos, Transgressions: Cultural Studies and Education is dedicated to exploring the ways cultural studies enhances the study and practice of education. With this in mind the series focuses in a non-exclusive way on popular culture as well as other dimensions of cultural studies including social theory, social justice and positionality, cultural dimensions of technological innovation, new media and media literacy, new forms of oppression emerging in an electronic hyperreality, and postcolonial global concerns. With these concerns in mind cultural studies scholars often argue that the realm of popular culture is the most powerful educational force in contemporary culture. Indeed, in the twenty-first century this pedagogical dynamic is sweeping through the entire world. Educators, they believe, must understand these emerging realities in order to gain an important voice in the pedagogical conversation.

Without an understanding of cultural pedagogy's (education that takes place outside of formal schooling) role in the shaping of individual identity – youth identity in particular – the role educators play in the lives of their students will continue to fade. Why do so many of our students feel that life is incomprehensible and devoid of meaning? What does it mean, teachers wonder, when young people are unable to describe their moods, their affective affiliation to the society around them. Meanings provided young people by mainstream institutions often do little to help them deal with their affective complexity, their difficulty negotiating the rift between meaning and affect. School knowledge and educational expectations seem as anachronistic as a ditto machine, not that learning ways of rational thought and making sense of the world are unimportant.

But school knowledge and educational expectations often have little to offer students about making sense of the way they feel, the way their affective lives are shaped. In no way do we argue that analysis of the production of youth in an electronic mediated world demands some "touchy-feely" educational superficiality. What is needed in this context is a rigorous analysis of the interrelationship between pedagogy, popular culture, meaning making, and youth subjectivity. In an era marked by youth depression, violence, and suicide such insights become extremely important, even life saving. Pessimism about the future is the common sense of many contemporary youth with its concomitant feeling that no one can make a difference.

If affective production can be shaped to reflect these perspectives, then it can be reshaped to lay the groundwork for optimism, passionate commitment, and transformative educational and political activity. In these ways cultural studies adds a dimension to the work of education unfilled by any other sub-discipline. This is what Transgressions: Cultural Studies and Education seeks to produce—literature on these issues that makes a difference. It seeks to publish studies that help those who work with young people, those individuals involved in the disciplines that study children and youth, and young people themselves improve their lives in these bizarre times.

There Is No Need to Talk about This

Poetic Inquiry from the Art Therapy Studio

Karen O. Wallace

SENSE PUBLISHERS
ROTTERDAM/BOSTON/TAIPEI

A C.I.P. record for this book is available from the Library of Congress.

ISBN: 978-94-6209-999-9 (paperback)
ISBN: 978-94-6300-000-0 (hardback)
ISBN: 978-94-6300-001-7 (e-book)

Published by: Sense Publishers,
P.O. Box 21858,
3001 AW Rotterdam,
The Netherlands
https://www.sensepublishers.com/

Printed on acid-free paper

All Rights Reserved © 2015 Sense Publishers

No part of this work may be reproduced, stored in a retrieval system, or transmitted in any form or by any means, electronic, mechanical, photocopying, microfilming, recording or otherwise, without written permission from the Publisher, with the exception of any material supplied specifically for the purpose of being entered and executed on a computer system, for exclusive use by the purchaser of the work.

To my Clients

TABLE OF CONTENTS

Introduction	xv
Chapter 1: What Is Art Therapy?	1
Talking about Art Therapy	2
Everyone Is an Artist	2
Why I Became an Art Therapist	3
When Play Is Therapy	4
Chapter 2: Art Therapy and Trauma	5
Sharp Edges	6
Learning to Wait	7
Boys Will Be Boys	7
Can Turn on a Dime	8
Power Play	8
Drawing	9
Disclosures	9
Retraumatization	9
Playing in the Sand	10
"What Does Cyrus Say?"	10
Be Here Now	12
Trigger Happy	12
Transition Time	13
Tricks of the Mind	14
Safe Landing	14
A Devastating Miracle	15
Chapter 3: Art Therapy and Dissociation	17
Coming Home to the Body	18
Promises	19
I Love It When You Laugh	19
Not Being Seen	20
Learning Restraint	20
Trained at Home	21
Prematurely Pushed	21
Chairs That I Have Known	22

TABLE OF CONTENTS

Does It Matter?	23
The Fires He Sets	23
This Moment	24
Shame	24
Because	24
Chapter 4: Art Therapy and Depression	27
My Client Has Depression	28
Abstract	29
Making the Darkness Go Away	30
She is Good at Drawing Faces	30
Sometimes It's the Art That Needs Healing	31
Homeward Bound	32
Old Beliefs	32
Lighting Candles	33
Teenagers	33
The Resistant Therapist	34
Mending	35
What the Picture Tells	35
Chapter 5: Art Therapy and Autism	37
She Thinks She Is Sonic the Hedgehog	38
Are You Human?	38
Is That All She Does, Just Play?	39
Secret Bridges	39
The Same as Last Week, Only Different	40
A Free Day	41
If Birds Can Fly, Why Oh Why, Oh Why Can't I?	41
Chapter 6: Art Therapy and Addiction	43
As Long as It Takes	44
The Right to Cut	45
Reaching Through the Layers	45
Afternoon Therapy	46
Staying in the Trenches	46
A Metaphor	47
What a Dangerous Bridge to Cross	47
On a Good Day	47
Edges of Knowing	48
It Wasn't Just	48
Not Enough	49

TABLE OF CONTENTS

Chapter 7: Art Therapy and Grief	51
Building Candy Castles	52
The Magic of Art	53
Dark Secrets	53
Fresh Beginning after Her Husband's Death	53
The Boy with the Beautiful Eyes	54
The Magic Cloth	54
Presence	55
Nests	56
Wanting Mom	56
A Make Over	57
The Sorrow of This Job	58
Missing	58
My Teacher	59
The Stories Not Told	61
Super Hero	62
Chapter 8: Art Therapy Groups and Honouring the Mother	63
Being a Mother	63
Hedgerow Teacher	64
A Bad Mother	64
What Is My Problem?	65
Resiliency: Missing Pieces	66
At 50	66
Don't Talk, Just Listen	67
Making Aprons	67
Hands	68
Chapter 9: Art Therapy Groups and Making Peace with Your Body	69
But I Am Fat ...	70
Paper Dolls	70
Snow White	71
You and Me	71
Body Maps	71
You Were Part of That Group	72
Body Blocked	72
Making Peace	73
Chapter 10: Art Therapy Groups and the Artful Archetypal Journey	75
A Poem about the Archetypal Group	76
Archetypal Drama	77

TABLE OF CONTENTS

Changing House	78
The Fool Archetype	80
We All Have the Right to Cast Spells	80
Those Who Know and Remember	81
The World Card	82
Chapter 11: Art Therapy Groups and Claiming Your Ruby Red Slippers	**83**
Looking behind the Curtain	84
Ruby Red Slippers	85
Deconstructing the Yellow Brick Road	85
Laying Down in the Field of Poppies	86
Safe Journey	86
Group Art	87
Chapter 12: Art Therapy Groups and Soul Garden	**89**
Recognizing Life	89
Prayer Flags	90
The Healing Touch of Nature	90
Seeds of Hope	91
Spirits	91
Moving through the Seasons	93
Chapter 13: Art Therapy Groups and Dream Work	**95**
Recurring Dreams	95
Dream-Work	96
Home Room	97
You Are Telling Me Your Nightmare	97
Childhood Dream	98
You Are Dreaming	98
Dream Circle	99
Duck Dreams	99
Chapter 14: Art Therapy Groups and Mindfulness	**101**
Being a Buddhist	102
Purity	103
It's Okay to Go in Circles	104
In-between	104
Witnessing	104
Meditating	104
Just Sitting	105
"Where's That Book?"	106

TABLE OF CONTENTS

Does He Have Your Back?	107
Grace	107
Chapter 15: Art Therapy Groups and a Place Like Home	**109**
Journey Home	110
Prairie Prayer	112
New Machines for the Same Old Practice	112
Forever Taking Leave	113
Your Time	114
Nothing Is Important	114
Brain Injury	114
Three Years Old	115
Grandma Brought You for Therapy	115
Shortcuts	116
Asking	116
Chapter 16: Art Therapy and Power of Transformation	**117**
Broken Images	118
Revision	118
Where Are You Now?	119
Be Here Now	120
The Artistic Mind	120
Mending a Broken Heart	120
The Power of Projection	121
Everyday Magic	121
Clichés	122
The Foster System	123
Wanting out	124
Closing	125
References	127

xiii

INTRODUCTION

Art Therapy and Creative Process

Therapy is solitary work. I think of it as a sacred process where someone is willing to open up, tell and show me their inner life. I listen, empathize, suggest, reflect and brainstorm with my clients about their past, present and imagined future life.

Clients come for different reasons, but most want change of some kind. I don't always know how change will happen, but it always does in some form. My poems are about change. Some speak to the messy, sticky part of it, and others talk of the joy and inspiration that often accompanies the process. Change can be scary, exalting, intimating and sometimes fun. My poems speak of knowing and understanding that process as I watch it work in others.

When I reflect on my therapy practice, I write poems. They help me process what happens. Change often happens subtly. Before it becomes explicit, some of my work requires interrupting, guiding, and being mindful and present with the birth of awareness or change. Often, clients have no idea how much work, cost and pain is demanded by change. I nurture and make visible an often invisible and very charged process. Changing deep emotional behaviour patterns formed over a lifetime is not easy. We humans don't easily let go of habituated feelings and patterns, even if they are painful and limiting.

My poems bear witness to my clients' deep desire for change, their belief that it can happen, commitment to the process and all the blocks, restrictions, struggles and fears that get in their way. I also explore their willingness to explore and face personal fears and anxieties. Change happens through dialogue, imagination, innovation, enlightenment, education, crisis, action, hope, inspiration, love, reflection and laughter. I strive to capture and reflect this complexity.

Some poems explain my work: how I see my clients, my job as an art therapist and my work in the therapy room. I share the range of different issues – from depression and abuse to trauma and body image. I talk about my art therapy groups and explain a bit of the process. These poems are small vignettes about what occurs in the therapy room.

None of these poems are about any individual or peculiar client. The poems are based on composites of the many clients that I have worked with over the many past years.

Some of my poems talk of home. A therapist's main job is to help the client to find and create a new way of being. It means feeling safe and secure in the here and now. I call this feeling "home", that is being grounded in the body and present. These poems explore what belonging means for people I work with.

INTRODUCTION

I also talk of personal therapy work, how I have healed my own wounds. If I want clients to attain a greater sense of wellbeing, health or wholeness, then I must also constantly do this work. I meditate, run, do yoga and write reflectively to increase my consciousness and wellbeing. I practice "focusing" (a process that involves tuning into myself) to ensure I am in touch with my emotional and mental work. Working on my own state of awareness is important in order to maximize my usefulness to others.

The focus of the therapy work is always on the whole, that is, how do I create wholeness out of what has been shattered? Who determines what wholeness looks like? We work with the complexity of what life gives us. Life experience informs and transforms us. In therapy, I help people make sense of and work with, not against, transformation. Can we ever really know anyone; can we ever know ourselves, and if so, which self? Who is asking the question? Can we ever know if people heal, why they do or don't?

I do not have answers, only observations. This is the essence of my practice and my poetry.

CHAPTER 1

WHAT IS ART THERAPY?

Therapy can be defined as a process that provides skills to solve life problems, heal emotional or psychological issues, and make life more enjoyable. Art therapy uses creativity to work with emotional, psychological and/or physical issues. It is about connecting with, accepting, communicating and acting from a deep, personal level. It is not about doing "good" art, as judgment is irrelevant. All that matters is whether it gives the client a new perspective, helps to get in touch with feelings and/or make changes.

Even if art is not pursued as therapy, creating art in itself is a healing, calming activity. Getting in the flow and connecting with our creative spirit is a healthy state.

Creating art helps create new perspectives, heal deep wounds and situates us in the here and now. My clients may create art as a way to settle or ground themselves to get ready for the session. Sometimes, after a long intense session involving Focusing, Somatic Experiencing or talk therapy, many clients use an art response as a way to close the experience. Others spend the whole session talking, drawing, painting or doing other art forms as they process memories, hurts, feelings of shame and guilt, or whatever they choose to work on. 'Art making' in therapy is a way of responding, going deeper into or reflecting what the client is experiencing, learning and understanding. New perspectives, insights or understanding cannot always be translated into words. We know formlessness through experiencing form, simplicity through complexity, eternity through experiencing limitation, freedom through experiencing entrapment. The stories I hear and images I see in therapy sessions reflect how each person is evolving through new perspectives. As clients work their way through the layers of being, I try to create breathing places, glimpses of the light, gaps in the human drama so that together, we can witness spirit shining through. Observing today's reality rather than resisting it helps one to see why we are here and become passionate about change as we stumble towards the light.

We enter the creative process when we reconnect deeply with our self. We each have a unique way of entering this process, of experiencing and drawing from it. When I give workshops on the creative process, we explore different art mediums, the art of "seeing," and find out what conditions encourage our creative process to bloom. Working in this way helps us move through trauma, loss, grief, and life transitions. Playing with art materials gives us the opportunity to explore creative unblocking and reframe old habits and ideas. In somatic art therapy, sensory work, meditation techniques, imagination, focusing, and art as play, the focus is on the process, not a finished product. Creating from this authentic place renews one's

CHAPTER 1

energy and vision, and guides one towards a deepening creative relationship with the self, which encourages self-growth, awareness, and self-understanding.

TALKING ABOUT ART THERAPY

I am asked to explain, "What is art therapy?" over and over again.

In my talks, how do I explain,
    That when someone is playing, creating art the imagination wakes up?
    And for an hour they are free of feeling stuck, depressed, and/or pain?

How to convey,
    That when someone is playing, creating art, the body relaxes lets go.
        And for an hour the anger, defenses and hurt
            Fall into flow, comfort and ease?

How do I open a window to show,
    That when someone is playing, creating art the mind frees up,
        And for an hour the circular thoughts, self-hatred, criticism,
            Give way to curiosity, wonder and clarity?

How do I explain,
    That when someone is playing, creating art, the emotions shift, balance,
        They experience joy, happiness and peace?

In my talks how do I explain,
    That this new way of being does not get lost, it becomes embodied.
        Slowly their lives become more creative and so full of colour,
            They can't remember what it was like before they had creative license.

How do I say all this,
    When Art Therapy is about being in the experience,
        Not talking about it?

EVERYONE IS AN ARTIST

I am arguing with my son,
Who says anybody can do art.
I say some people are afraid.
I say some people are horrified
If they were to pick up a brush
And dip it in paint.
They would find themselves frozen
In front of the blank, white canvas
And feel foolish,

WHAT IS ART THERAPY?

Wanting to disappear.
Or immediately remember
That their grade eight teacher
Told them trees did not look
Like that or that their grade one
Teacher told them they could not cut,
Paste, or draw.

My son says that most people don't experience that.
And I insist I'm an art therapist;
I hear people's problems all day.
I say, "what if someone told you that
You were not creative and that
You couldn't paint right or that you
Should learn a trade because you weren't going to
make it as an artist?"
"What if someone said, 'Get serious.
It's a tough world. Get a real job.'"
Then he said, "You wouldn't have let me get
a real job. You don't have one."
I tried to keep a straight face.

WHY I BECAME AN ART THERAPIST

When I thought about why I became an Art Therapist,
I always thought it was because I was depressed and started to make candles and somehow the making of candles; working with the melting wax, forming the shapes, designing the colours, saved me from the dark hole that had claimed me.
That memory always seemed pivotal and important.
But recently, other memoires have been surfacing,
Seeming so obvious and ordinary that I can't believe that I over looked them.
Neighbouring farmers were always dropping in to visit Dad.
Talking, sometimes drinking beer in the milk house from the old fridge.
My five year old self thought they talked about cows, lack of rain, or how high the corn had grown,
but now I think it was therapy.
Dad listening, offering advice, maybe about bad marriages, or controlling fathers that would not move off the farms that these men now worked.
And they always came at dinnertime, which made Mom mad.
And there were other things that make me think that it was Dad.
The memory of a young boy who somehow had ran all the way from his farm to ours which stood high on a hill and Dad talking to him in the kitchen and getting him cookies and milk.

3

CHAPTER 1

A few hours later a red truck showed up to take him home, after Dad talked to the father in a loud voice about it better not happen again.
And a boy a few houses away from ours, nonverbal, brain injured, coming and sitting in our kitchen and Dad would let him, no questions asked.
And Charlie, a second cousin who I would see walking up our long lane way to sit in the same chair, as did many others.
Somehow these people knew he was a safe anchor in their troubled lives.
Now, after many years of being a therapist, I realize that the journey of reinvention can take any shape; a walk up a kind farmers laneway, a cab ride to an Art Therapists Studio, or a trip to a hair stylist.
And those who practice the art of re-imagination can be anyone who is brave enough to say yes, in a brutal world.

WHEN PLAY IS THERAPY

My younger cousin, born late in a marriage that already contained two girls and two boys, and I would play every Sunday when our families drove down those windy, dusty roads to the lake.
We made villages under the trees and acorn families and leaf furniture and had to be called long and hard before we could hear the adults below interrupting our world for something as trite as dinner.
My aunt would thank me for baby-sitting him and I would look at her like she was crazy because before he came along, no one spoke my language or understood the magic of play, the way he did.

CHAPTER 2

ART THERAPY AND TRAUMA

Most of the clients that I write about have experienced high levels of trauma at early ages. A life experience becomes traumatic when a person cannot integrate the emotions, bodily sensations and/or thoughts that result from a frightening, life threatening or shocking experience. This means that they have little or no knowledge of how to calm themselves when faced with overwhelming thoughts or feelings. Never having developed the ability to self regulate, they find themselves struggling with ordinary life experiences expecting and perceiving everyone and everything as a threat. In the poem *Sharp Edges* I talk about a boy who through making art and trusting the creative process learned to slow down enough to allow his autonomic nervous system to start healing. Our close relationship and making art helped him heal his emotional detachment and dissociation that years of living in trauma had produced.

The poem *Learning to Wait* talks about a girl who suffered physical, mental and emotionally abuse. It is often slow work, getting through layers of trauma and releasing the repetitive patterns of reliving and remembering traumatic memories, and suffering from the symptoms. Often if abuse victims do not understand that their violation was not their fault, they have a difficult time developing self-esteem and resilience. I see a wide range of reactions to, and symptoms of, trauma.

However, for all clients there are flashbacks or reoccurring memories of all or some parts of painful situations that caused the client to go into fight or flight.

Trauma triggers could be people who look like the abuser, places that are similar to where a traumatic event happened or things, which the client associates with the trauma memory that act as reminders of the original traumatic event and show where the client is stuck or unable to move forward in their life. The poems *Boys will be Boys* and *Drawing* describe how triggers reappear for clients and how in drawings or paintings clients can find a safe way to explore, get distance from and start processing the images. These images and memories highjack the client and keep them locked in fear. In Art and/or Play Therapy we can safely work with triggers in a transformative way.

Traumatization is a poem about a girl I worked with for several years. Play therapy for her allowed conflict, fear or trauma to be re-experienced, resolved and integrated. Re-experienced means that the client is painting about, drawing or sewing about the experience. I am there as a support, witness and resource, centred in the part of the client that feels strong enough to meet this traumatized other place that dwells inside and release some of the emotion and pain.

CHAPTER 2

As clients learn to be creative and expressive, creating art also offers an opportunity to memorialize losses and connect with others. The creating and making of art in itself is a healing and therapeutic process. Many physical and psychological skills are learned through making and processing art images. A byproduct of working in art is that clients gain a stronger sense of who they are and what they are capable of achieving in the world. Art Therapy combines art and psychotherapy in a creative process using the created image as a foundation for self-exploration and understanding.

What does Cyrus say? speaks about working with an individual who suffers from a mental disorder due to his prolonged exposure to stress and trauma as a child. Prolonged exposure causes many physiological problems such as a weak immune system, heart and blood pressure problems, and brain damage. Extreme stress in early years of life can disrupt normal development of the hippocampus. PTSD (post traumatic stress disorder), results when trauma goes untreated. This individual had all the symptoms of PTSD which means he lived in a world where he relived his trauma daily, had intense fears and high emotional numbing. Play Therapy for him was life changing. He had not had a normal childhood where he was allowed to play, dream, and imagine. In this safe environment he slowly unravelled his stories of childhood abuse and suffering.

Triggers is a poem about the pain and confusion that trauma causes. Traumatized individuals often act out in inappropriate ways because they are in high amounts of pain and can't self regulate. This behaviour can be misdiagnosed in harmful ways. The girl I was writing about suffered from abandonment issues, substance abuse, dissociation and PTSD. Through Art Therapy she began understanding why her behaviour was so chaotic, it became possible for her to start learning how to self regulate and to stop reacting. Self-mutilation, depression, and anger are often the result of unresolved trauma.

Tricks of the Mind and *Safe Landing* are conversations I had with clients as they paint, work with clay or draw. Sometimes this creating happens in silence when I am more of a support and witness. Sometimes we both create beside each other. Sometimes my client works on a project that takes several weeks and we are talking as they work away with their hands, piecing together what was broken.

SHARP EDGES

The hope I didn't know that I was waiting for
Just walked through the door
In the shape of a teenage boy
Angry, lost, shut down,
Hard-edged as a scalpel probing an open wound.

And I kept thinking how making art
Travels the path of least resistance,

How it cuts through steel and stone

When no one is looking, probing into a teenage boy's business,
It can blast through years of emptiness, mistrust
Breaking open the body above the rubble,
Raw feelings emerge.

And sharp edges turn into wanting hot chocolate
And checking cupboards for new art supplies
I saw, out from under the toughness, a small
Innocent boy excited at the attention,
And loving the chance to play.

LEARNING TO WAIT

My client and I are talking about love.

She says that she believes a person can love someone
And still be able to physically hurt them.

I say, "That's not love. That's co-dependence."
She says, "No, that's love. You can love someone, and be so
angry at them that you hurt them."

I say, "Then it's not love anymore."
She says, "Love doesn't have rules."

I say, "I'm not sure we mean the same thing when we say love."
She says, "People are messed up: Love exists in that mess."

I say that what she might mean by love is desire.
"Love is not a feeling," I say. And she says, "Then what is it?"

I try to sort through the sappy answers and come up with something brilliant, right, or at least decent. I say that I think she means hope; love is hope.

She tells me I don't know what she thinks, and I agree.

What I really mean is that I love her too much to have her think that hurt could ever be part of love, so how could I allow broken arms, black eyes?

We both know it's not up to me.
So I wait.

BOYS WILL BE BOYS

Here we sit, drinking tea and talking about how the week has been,
Me, asking you my questions.

CHAPTER 2

Soon enough, you reveal a childhood story from second grade,
The one about when others punched and kicked until the bell rang,
And your face, frozen lost in the memory, still numb from the beating.

I can see in you the 8-year-old, wanting it to be over;
Caught in a story embodied as a wound that bubbles up begging for release,
Afraid that, once again it will see the playground bully.

CAN TURN ON A DIME

A hairstylist once had cards made up for everyone in the salon,
Each card containig interesting facts about them on the flip side.
His said, "Can turn on a dime."
I was never quite sure what that meant.

A few weeks ago, I was followed.
He could have been going in the same direction.
It was raining, broad daylight, no need to panic.

Dimes are the smallest coin in the U.S.A.
"Can turn on a dime," means to change direction quickly,
To turn in a small space, or to make a tight turn.
I guess Todd could change directions fast.
I don't know how it applied to him.

He cornered me, closed in, was ready to assault,
When I turned on a dime.
I confidently, calmly escaped.
He tried to follow,
But, apparently, did not have the right change.

POWER PLAY

I know this desolate place,
You and I in the therapy room,
With despair wrapped around, trying to pull us down.
You struggle with not wanting to let go of the feelings that have wrestled you under,
But I made a raft out of scraps of hope.

I know the power and play of reinventing the self after a bad childhood,
And this is what you have come for.
Your painful memories are starting to realize how futile it is to resist.

DRAWING

You were drawing the man who molested you when you were 5,

On small sheets of paper and getting closer and closer to seeing his face,

When, finally, he appeared.

You felt you had to see him once again to get past it.

But somehow the image bled through into your morning coffee and nighttime television:

You worried that he was everyone and everything you knew.

We worked together to capture him once more on the paper, and slowly he turned whiter and whiter then disappeared.

You would run your hand over his absent image making sure he was gone.
And I kept you busy with the future so you wouldn't see faint outlines.

DISCLOSURES

Nothing quite prepares your mind for the sudden disclosures.

The way a child can open up a story that barrels down with a punishing speed that almost knocks you flying.

And as you continue playing, trying to stay calm and collected,

Slowly becoming aware of the weight of the words,

and your new responsibility in having caught their meaning.

Realizing that after she leaves you have to phone her worker, report what

she said without any certainty of what kind of new beginning this means for her.

And as your body submits to the task,

your mind is twisting and bending to make sure that there isn't a way out,

Because you know she can't take another move to another strange address.

RETRAUMATIZATION

You are captured by your dead foster mother, again.

Telling anyone who will listen about being tied up in the basement.

Laughing about the door sticker that was your friend on those lonely nights,

CHAPTER 2

And maybe days.

It's been 10 years and the memories are fresh, but messy.

The one thing you want to know is how could she have done that?
Tied you up, fed you baby food, and made you wear a dog collar?

As you come and go in and out of the basement,
I try to poke holes in the looping memories.

I reassure you, it's over and you're never going back there,
As you plead to return.

I search for windows and doors in your mind that will help you escape,
And sometimes I find one, but she always manages to pull you back to her
And tie you to that chair.

We ran out of there together, you and I in my art therapy studio,
Holding hands all the way to Regina, where she can't find you.

But all it takes is the wrong look from someone, a smell,
And she has got you again.

And we start all over, with me trying to throw lifelines,
Through emergency exits that you keep opening, just in case.

PLAYING IN THE SAND

She silently, slowly, placed characters face down in the sand

As she spoke,

This is my father, my mother, my sister, my brother,

Me in the middle,

All asleep.

How else could these things happen to me at night?

In a sane world this would make sense.

"WHAT DOES CYRUS SAY?"

Once a week he comes for Play Therapy.
And we bowl.

We don't always bowl. He used to reenact his tortured childhood in the sandtray, paint about his rage and make clay figures representing the boys who bullied him.

But now, we have settled into a world between my couch and fridge that is the bowling alley.

It's a tough competition between Dave, me, and my dog Cyrus.

Cyrus is usually the early leader, and although Dave bowls for him, he is usually worried that this time Cyrus may win.

"What's Cyrus saying Karen?" asks Dave. And I say, "Cyrus is saying 'I can't believe that I am beating Dave!'"

The faces that I have glued to the fridge to help teach children what different emotions look like, cheer when Dave gets a strike, and laugh when Dave hits the pins into the cabinets.

All the stuffed animals take turns commenting on the game when Dave randomly picks one and ask what they are saying.

And the bowling pins talk. But the one with the most to say is the red pin. "What is the red pin saying Karen?" asks Dave.

It's saying, 'why do I always have to be racked up first? Why do I always have to take the full force of Dave's wicked throws?' And the other pins say, 'be quiet. We all feel the strength of Dave's thunder balls.'

And Dave laughs, because the red pin always complains and the other pins are always telling it to be quiet.

And Dave has thunder balls, and lightening balls, and thunder fireballs, and tornado balls. Dave watches the weather station and I always ask him what the weather will be like on the weekend.

And once in awhile during the game, Dave will ask, "Can I tell you something?" and I say "Yes Dave, what?" and then I wait because it takes awhile. But this is also why he is here. For these brief, quiet moments of telling me something from the past, the imagined future or the present. A memory about his hometown, a story about his imaginary brother or what happened at school today.

"Tell Cyrus the score Karen." Dave says. I say, "Cyrus, Dave is at 300 points, you are next with 280 and I am in the rear at 200." Dave says, "What did Cyrus say?" I say 'Wow, Dave is the King of the Bowling Alley!' and Dave smiles his little sweet smile and tells me for the hundredth time as he lines up his next throw, "Watch and learn Karen, watch and learn."

And in this world of dogs who bowl and stuffed toys and pictures that can come alive, Dave is always the winner.

CHAPTER 2

BE HERE NOW

We were having dinner with friends who are therapists.
Ronald announced he was moving to Africa
To work with traumatized children.
"I don't want to work with middle-class, Oak Bay clients anymore,
I want to really make a difference."
That's the new anthem for therapists:
"Let's go to Africa" or, failing that,
Any traumatized war zone will do,
Anywhere that will drown out White privilege.
I lamely argue the impossibility
Of qualifying a person's trauma, pain, or wounding.
"How can you judge if a child in Africa,
Has more need of your White, middle-class training as therapist,
Than has a child in Oak Bay who just saw his brother commit suicide?"

The words were as unpopular as if I had said,
"Angelina and Brad should stop adopting babies."

I worked in the school system with a counselor who had given up years ago.
I did art therapy with seven children a day; he filed reports,
Hid on the phone, made cynical remarks at team meetings.
When last I saw him, he was going to volunteer in Africa,
"To make a difference."
Here, children's problems were their middle-class upbringing, their material wealth.
I tried to converse about making change where we are.
"If we can't make a change with the children we work with,
Can we really make change anywhere?
Who really needs change? the people we work with? or us, therapists?
Who determines what the change should look like?"
You know, the conversation us middle-class, White therapists can afford to have.
Maybe Angelina and Brad are on to something with the multicultural approach:
There has to be a child, somewhere, who can make us feel whole.

TRIGGER HAPPY

I am working with a fifteen year old,

Explaining triggers;

Those things that cause you to go into fight or flight,

Events that spark your reptilian brain to jump into action preparing you for battle,

Only there is no battle.

Just a memory replay activated by a hand on your shoulder,

A man standing too close.

But the brain cannot distinguish from past or present and

All you know is that your body is in danger mode,

And you will do whatever you need to do to survive.

But your high school teacher does not know about trauma theory,

That your body had been hijacked by memories,

All she sees is an angry, aggressive girl who,

Explodes when people come to close,

And she wants this behaviour to stop.

So, you are sent to me with the diagnosis of impulsive anger disorder

And we start the long journey back through the years;

All the nights when you couldn't defend yourself,

And all the times when your body wanted to fight

But couldn't, not against someone three times your size.

We release the built up tension and pain your brain has been storing all these years,

Slowly the fog of dissociation that was protecting you lifts,

You are transported into the present moment,

Your feet firmly planted on the ground,

Your frozen emotions fluid again,

You have to begin the arduous journey of being here now,

Where trust is still a mystery.

TRANSITION TIME

Transition: to move smoothly from one activity to another, one room to another or one life to another.

CHAPTER 2

The children I work with are said to have trouble with transitions. Their report cards are laced with remarks like, "Can't transition well; Cannot negotiate transitions" or my favourite, "Has a transition deficit".

In my therapy space, in the transition time: between art activities, or when the Social Worker has arrived to take them home and has me engaged in conversation, or when I turn my head for three minutes to get a missing tool, is the ripe time to stick small objects in pockets.

The children that I work with who have fallen out of being on time, who can't fit into structured time, are always looking for the right time when no one is looking, are trying to find a rhythm that matches their inward feelings of being out of time.

That is why when I watched Joe stick a Lego piece in his pocket last week, this time I turned my head and pretended that I didn't see.

TRICKS OF THE MIND

I am following the paintbrush that is marking this canvas,
With bright colours.

Marveling at the freedom that always begins a painting,
Then seeing it stop, and turn into harsh questions,
Over the shape of the face.

Not good enough, doesn't look right.
A frozen, stiff fear enters the room, and what was once fun,
Now becomes a place of doubt and shame.

Outward, beyond the studio where my client limits herself into a corner,
A new picture beckons filled with wide open prairie fields,
And a baby blue sky, cutting through the frozen fear of mistake making
And in wingback chairs we sit and paint.

Free of the mind's relentless watching for what is not right,
We paint, knowing that we are living on borrowed time.

SAFE LANDING

You and I in the therapy room,
You diving head first into the darkness,
Me treading water trying to find ground that will hold.

You apologize and say you wish it didn't have to be like this,
Me knowing that death in this moment would feel better than bearing witness to what you have just experienced.

I watch you struggle with not wanting to let go of the drama that has you by the throat.

The trick in the shift. It must be done as tenderly as holding a trembling, panicking baby that feared you would never come to stop the feelings of hunger and loneliness.

The despair is still here in this room, nothing has changed about its need, but now it has a soft arm wrapped around it and a chance to catch its breath.

The screaming has stopped.

A DEVASTATING MIRACLE

They all want babies.
Come from broken families.

Somehow they believe (these young girls I counsel 13 years old or so)
That a baby will heal the loss, mend the wound, and create that space where everything comes together and they live happily ever after….

And I have seen it happen. Young confused, heart broken girls who give birth and all a sudden they are transformed into awakened beings who "get it" and absent mothers come back and silent fathers speak once again and relatives send money.

But the Social Workers tell them that they will take away the babies because they are 'unfit, too young" and girls get pregnant anyway because even though they are wards of the state, their workers do not hide under their beds.

And me? I make dolls with the girl whose baby died in the womb at four months so we can talk about grief; and a necklace to release the feelings of loss with the mom, using the ultra sound picture of the baby who died at six months; and I talk to Anne about how hard it is to be up all night with a crying baby but, I understand how much she wants one.

And I try to explain that having a baby will not heal the loneliness, the lack of belonging, and hole in their hearts and stomachs. But I get it; the longing, the urge to hold a new fresh being, to heal what was broken. We all want that.

And who are we to tell these girls what will heal them? We do not live their joy, their desire, or their pain. But, maybe a child will be that devastating miracle that can do that.

CHAPTER 3

ART THERAPY AND DISSOCIATION

In my work I see many different degrees and varieties of dissociation as psychological numbing, disengagement and/or amnesia. When most people experience trauma, they suffer some degree of dissociation (i.e., a distance or a sense of separation from bodily sensations, emotions, and/or thoughts). When we experience overwhelming pain or events, our body disassociates, or separates, from the event or feelings and, at the time, it keeps us safe. But problems result when this mechanism becomes habitual, blocking awareness of sensations in the body through habits of dissociation and repression.

We separate from the inner knowing and awareness of the body and distance ourselves from uncomfortable or painful sensations and feelings. The poem *Coming Home to the Body* speaks of the problem that occurs when we dissociate from our body and no longer feel that we have a home or anchor in which to situate or place the 'self'. Dissociating from our bodies, or no longer feeling that it is safe to have bodily sensations or feel our feelings, means that we are always on guard, anxious, nervous or in a state of flight or fight.

Dissociation can happen when a child is placed in any new situation such as a new foster home or school. Any new explained event signals the body to dissociate so the child or adult may escape pain. The poem *Not Being Seen* talks about a child's experience of school trauma. Often dissociation is misdiagnosed as learning disabilities, or other problems when really the child is reliving past trauma. *Chairs that I have Known* speaks to how familiar objects, smells and/or sights can bring on the dissociate state.

Some of the responses of dissociation are feeling numb, detached, or a sense of de-realization. Time is often experience as suspended. Some clients experience psychosis and others faint often. The poem *Trained at Home* is about a girl who came from a violent and abusive home and had learned to detach from her life experience almost completely. Her face would go blank when I first started talking about her family and I would watch her withdraw into her fantasy world, which we eventually started to make tangible and real. Through Art and Play Therapy we could talk about the intense trauma that she had experienced and bring her fantasy world out of the dreamlike secretive world into the real setting of my Art Studio.

We all use dissociative mental mechanisms all the time as in daydreaming. That is not harmful. Dissociation becomes harmful to the body and mind when it becomes a primary adaptive response and takes over as in the poems *Prematurely Pushed* and *Does it Matter?*

CHAPTER 3

Usually the adaptive response of the children that I work with is a mixture of hyper-arousal and dissociation. *The Fire He Sets* is about a boy who would demonstrate extreme violent and dissociate behaviour. He was always in a state of high alert, but would look at me blankly with no emotional response. His answers were always evasive and unfocused. He had a history of being sexually abused from a young age and those memories become stored in lower parts of the brain. Any direct or indirect reminders of his early abuse would result with him acting violently although he had dissociated himself from those early memories. Part of the healing work that we did together was to bring these unconscious memories into his conscious awareness so that he did not need to withdraw into himself in order to survive.

Transformation of trauma involves the acknowledgment and the knowing of the inner movement of sensation. This energy and awareness are essential in reconnecting what has been fragmented by trauma. Fragmented aspects involve disorganized, interconnecting systems. Reconnection can occur when one stays in the conscious sensation long enough to experience both the discomfort of the unresolved trauma, as well as the vital, healing life force. The poem *This Moment* talks about working with a girl who was beginning to be able to stay in her body when we worked with her past trauma. She was starting to gain the inner resources and strengths to not use dissociation when she started to feel fear.

COMING HOME TO THE BODY

Perhaps (or not) anywhere can be home.
How do meanings of being 'at home' become encoded in the body?
When we are at home in our bodies,
Are we not home wherever our bodies are?

But where are we who don't call the body home?
When the body is unfamiliar, unsafe?
Our complex self can negotiate our sense of belonging
To be somewhere else—homeless.
Much can be missed when there's no body to come home to.

Being a nomad forces one to relocate continuously,
Depending on the space found, the weather, the seasons.
One's very survival depends on mobility … move or die.
The 'lived body' can contract, expand whenever it needs,
To shape to the immediate situation.

Perhaps (or not) anywhere can be home.
A static body sometimes needs to be interrupted,
Shaken free of attachments,
Moved to new places, homes, and experiences.
But a homeless, nomadic body gets tired, ill, loses shape,
Having nothing to connect to; no place to rest; to settle; to be.

PROMISES

Yesterday in the Art therapy Studio Ron wanted to know how to sew a stuffed animal that we had talked about last time and I was tired because everybody else had done paintings, clay and crafts and I did not want to drag out the machine because it was 5:30PM and I told him that I had to think about it.

But this morning after Joe made scenes in the sand tray and Jena was journaling and Brenda painting, I remembered how many times they all hear no and live with broken promises and I remembered why it was important to make the effort even when I don't feel like it.

I LOVE IT WHEN YOU LAUGH

Sometimes it frightens me, your laughter sounding manic and out of control. Certainly not centred or grounded.

But at least it is laughter and not the violent outbursts that you express when you are depressed and angry.

One extreme or the other, and the experts in their white coats really don't know what to do.

So, they are constantly adjusting your drugs and trying something new, that might help or heal or wake you up from wherever and whatever it is that stalks you.

And for some reason, Art Therapy, seems to help, for now.
And for awhile during each hour, you are glad to be here, wanting a do a craft, talk, play and then you start pacing, worrying about when your worker is coming to pick you up.

And for awhile during each hour, your collection of fears, never far from you, trying to sneak up and take over, I can coax to wait by the door so we can have our hour of uninterrupted time.

And for awhile during each hour, your floating body, disconnected and filled with crippling fear, I can convince to settle, soften, and come an inch closer so we can have our hour of uninterrupted time.

And for awhile during each hour, your small, tight self coiled up in loneliness, I can convince to stretch out and breathe, and trust that no one will hurt it, so we can have our hour of uninterrupted time.

And when your worker does come to take you back to your group home,
She asks you,"Did you have fun?" Because she can't see the broken chains of fear on the floor or smell the courage you have been using to fight your history of pain.

CHAPTER 3

And you laugh, that beautiful laugh.

NOT BEING SEEN

When I first went to school,
I couldn't believe my sister was going to leave me there
Alone in that classroom, with a teacher who couldn't see me.
It was only 6 miles from home, but it was a foreign country:
I couldn't speak the language, know the customs, or understand the rules.
I faded into No Man's Land.

Once, Patrick and I camped between Morocco and Algeria
In a small, narrow strip called No Man's Land,
Because we were not allowed in either country.
Guards walked by with guns; feral dogs barked at night.
I often felt like that in school.
I lost my landmarks of belonging:
The farm fields I walked in, my stonewall and
Tin box filled with poems,
And our playhouse, once a chicken coup.
It wasn't until Grade 6 that a teacher saw me
Wandering and coaxed me to come in.
She must have seen something in me,
Perhaps an earlier version of herself.
Regardless, I made sure I stayed close to the edge of belonging
Because I did not trust this building.
I hadn't found my home, but I found an open door.

LEARNING RESTRAINT

He starts out like any other kid, playful, happy, dreamy.

And then it builds, his face going blank, and just before he resembles a keg of dynamite ready to explore,

I get him to practice pausing, slowing down for a split second so he can have the restraint that his father (who beat him nightly) never got the chance to develop.

He stands there angry, fists tight, glaring at me but not acting on his usual impulse to take a swing and I slowly talk him into a softer place that lies under the rage.

A place that he has fought hard to keep caged up but I get him to visit his underlying vulnerability that so desperately wants his attention.

And as we keep his anguish and vulnerability company, he tells me about how he wanted to kill his dad when night after night he had to absorb his rage.

And slowly his hot energy cools, we sit down. There are no longer any words, just him trusting me that I may know the way out.

TRAINED AT HOME

She was four, referred to me because of extreme
Behaviour problems at pre-school.

I wondered about her home life and, as we started therapy,
Found that in her home no one quarrelled. Instead,

They had learned to be silent, learned to nod,
Learned to wear the cloak of shame and anger of abuse.

She was unassailable, unmovable, adamant
Her father was nice; he played nice; home was nice,
Everything and everyone was nice.

I marvelled at her expressionless face and
Rote answers that therapeutic games, questioning, drawing, and
Movement could not penetrate.

She was not going to break into tears and shouts,
Let loose a river of lament, let us in on the Secret.

They, families like her's,
Learned centuries ago how to keep
The neighbours, the therapists, the social workers,
And the nosey teachers, who saw bruises, out of their business.

She could still come to my art therapy studio,
Learn the healing of talk, the calming of art making,
And the peace of attention.

And I know that even in this cacophonic chorus,
We find a ritual of living the best we can.

PREMATURELY PUSHED

Due to shocking acts of violence, some of my clients and I have places in our bodies that feel empty, vacated.

Buddha talked about having to go through the gates of emptiness to find true existence.

CHAPTER 3

The open space where raw pulsing creative energy waits to come into form.

And maybe, this is where we were prematurely pushed and forced to enter into this scared ground before we could language it.

Now, don't confuse this poem with absolution for the one who shoved us here by knifepoint. I know that there are gentler, kinder ways.

But, you and I, through the paradox of abuse being a doorway to healing, ended up here.
And surrounding this holy space stand other parts of me, the Wounded One, the Angry One, and the Trembling One and they are all welcome.

They are key players in deciding the direction of this story. Will they bow to pain and suffering or will they point the way to grace? There are many ways home.

CHAIRS THAT I HAVE KNOWN

When I was little, I escaped into the pictures found in books.
One of my favourite pictures to come home to, to find home in,
And to live through,
Was of a rustic little cottage, with a wonderful hand-made chair.

I loved that chair – a rough little chair – with a cushion stuffed with straw,
Painted yellow.
I sat for hours (so it seemed) and imagined living in that cottage,
With that chair.
Years later, in our home on Pender Island,
My partner made me a 'Queen of the Woods' chair
That looked a lot like that chair in my little book,
The chair, that was Home.

I naively walk into the old farm kitchen,
Now inhabited by my brother and his family,
Trying to stay intact.
Already fading, I scan the light, dusty blue of this well-worn room
And my eyes rest on the bulky, overstuffed,
Aged, blue-and-light-brown-plaid chair in the corner.

The rancid, musky animal smells of the farm where I grew up
Start penetrating my melting armour, getting deep into my skin.
The filtered light coming through the small lace curtains
Tied back in-the-middle with ribbons,
Makes me feel light-headed as I step back
Into the old, familiar fading feeling of 'not being here.'

Exhausted, not even putting up a fight, I surrender into the chair
Feeling the fabric itchy on the back of my legs
I am instantly embraced by the past.
I am, once again, homeless.

DOES IT MATTER?

Does it matter that one more First Nations child is lost in the system?
She was so thin to start with.
Just another child using up taxpayers dollars and where would she end up anyway?
On the street, in the bars, just another drunk Indian.

Does it matter that the last time she came for art therapy
She would not hug me, but remained stiff as a board
When I tried to put my arms around her,
Knowing that I would be one more person who would be taken away from her?

Does it matter that when I asked her,
How she felt about not being able to go back to her foster home,
She told me she had no feelings.
And she stood there, all of 8 years old, knowing no one wanted her.

THE FIRES HE SETS

I see him in the fires he sets.

His soft blue mysterious under glow,
His angry reds and oranges.

His tremendous trapped energy that breaks out into flames,
Burning down abandoned barns and the neighbour's bushes.

His bold recklessness pours out like the lighter fluid,
Spilling onto his shirt just before he struck the match.

And his secrets, shame, and dark thoughts that reappear like phoenixes rising from the ashes.

My job? As I spin in circles not knowing where to point the water:
Is to follow the underground trail of silent hints,
All the while not knowing where he will throw the next match.

I want to show him how his fire can be the cure,
Not the trouble that escorts him to the police station.

But right now, he is more fascinated with the sounds of the sirens.

CHAPTER 3

THIS MOMENT

This moment makes up for all the confusion and struggle.
The two of us happy, walking Cyrus my dog, care free talking about which houses we would live in, musing about how Cyrus could never catch the squirrels that taunt her, and me laughing at Cyrus licking your face.

In this moment I am not trying to help you redirect your anger, or release your trauma. In this moment we are free, moving forward with no traces of the sadness, grief or pain that usually accompany our time together.

I want to memorize your smile, the ease of your replies, the ordinariness of our walk. It is a simple scene, yet nuanced with possibilities.
The two of us on a walk with a dog, adrift in happiness.

SHAME

A girl I work with was making a dream catcher and could not wrap and pull the leather cord tight around the ring, threw it onto the art table in frustration.

I had been making one along side her and I slipped mine into her hands with gentle soothing words about first time being hard and until I had made three or four I couldn't get the rhythm of it. And she continued to work as I watched the cloak of shame that had turned her mouth into a tight line and eyes cold slip to the floor.

BECAUSE

Because she had changed.

Because she laughed differently, harder, somehow a bit mean.

Because after being in foster homes all summer, she was returned home.

Because she was sad, but pretended everything was O.K.

Because she was returned, but her sister wasn't.

Because everyone in the family hurt, were in pain.

Because they had to go on making breakfasts, attend school, and drive to Regina for groceries.

Because they wanted things to be normal again.

Because they thought they knew what 'normal' looked like, but she would have nothing to do with it.

Because when she was in a foster home,

Praying to go back to her family,
She and I made wishes with the crystal wand,
But when I pulled it out last week she said,
"Put that away, it doesn't work."

CHAPTER 4

ART THERAPY AND DEPRESSION

Working with the sorrows of the psyche is similar to working with sorrows of the flesh. If you have a cut, you don't immediately change it, make it into something else. You meet it where it is. You listen to your body, find out what it needs to heal and tenderly give it what it needs. The cut starts to heal itself with your support. And you trust that it will continue.

Depression needs listening, gentle caring, and holding. Depression is a state of sadness, anxiousness, emptiness, hopelessness, helplessness and/or worthlessness. Often clients experience loss of appetite or overeat, have problems concentrating and remembering, contemplate suicide, experience insomnia or sleep excessively.

These stories are about my experience of working with clients in their times of darkness. *My Client Has Depression* talks about the darkness, suffering, and despair that this condition can bring.

Childhood depression is a relatively new diagnosis. *Abstract* talks about a child who was severely depressed. Before she came to Art Therapy she hadn't had a chance to talk about her childhood in a safe environment. This silence resulted in depression. When we don't accept the darkness, there is nothing to reflect the light. My clients have taught me that acceptance alone of whatever is present – depression, fear, shame – is enough to allow re-alignment or resolution in the body and creates forward movement. It stops the mental or emotional resistance that keeps the body locked in the condition. Acceptance of feelings, behaviours, and/or thoughts frees the body to move to new feelings, behaviours, and thoughts. Non-acceptance sets up resistance or locks the body into rigidity. When we don't accept the 'all that is there' the body resists moving forward.

In *Making the Darkness Go Away* I am questioning our desire as a society to pathologize everything. I talk about finding our way with sadness, unhappiness, and making whatever we need along the way to help, maybe hanging beads that reflect the light so the darkness has a normal, healthy, and realistic way to be in our lives. Art Therapy can be used to find a way of accepting and working with what is, in a creative way. We need to stop trying to block the way with diagnosis, meds, theories, and fear.

Sometimes little girls have nothing to smile about. We can't push the darkness away without also losing the light.

Homeward Bound and *Old Ideas* come from conversations with older clients that have lived with depression for most of their lives. In the first poem, my client was raised with a mother who was depressed. Depression can be caused from genetic

CHAPTER 4

vulnerability and developmental experiences where children are exposed to a depressed parent and or trauma. Children who are raised in an atmosphere where the adults around them think and feel in a negative, depressive context can model this and develop depressive symptoms.

Lighting Candles is a poem that I wrote about working with a woman whose depression was relentless and didn't ever seem to lift for long. *Mending* speaks of a client's hope that she may be able to start a new life, one free of the darkness that plagues her.

MY CLIENT HAS DEPRESSION

Depression keeps her locked up in her apartment repeating the most shameful cruel things she has ever said about herself over and over again until she is deep in the hole of despair.

She has heard it all before, but each time the words hit freshly with new promises that this time she will scratch the bottom of her self-hatred and somehow crawl her way up to the top.

Then for no apparent reason, some days are better. She can use her meditation, positive affirmations and journal writing, all the things we talked about in the therapy room. It helps. But the good days feel like an out-of-body experience, like she is watching her life play out from behind a secret one-way mirror. Believing her real self is trapped down there.

She can't appreciate the highs as feeling good about her writing or having an enjoyable night with friends, because nothing feels real or good enough with the depression always lurking in the background ready to remind her that she can't process what is happening because she can't be completely sure it's happening at all.

It tugs at her skirt when a small mistake happens or feelings of being left out because her friends are having coffee and she was not invited. It drops her crying on the floor because she is tired and hungry and she has trouble sleeping and she is too tired to go for a walk. It pushes on those hurt feelings until they manifest into uncontrollable anxiety and simple tasks become undoable and all she can think about is the million of ways that she does not belong. And she can't explain it because it is all too vague. She does not want to disappoint or worry all the people who believe in her. Everyone who thought she was smart, creative and fearless.

As she slips down into the haze of depression, she can still feel the need to be productive like she used to, but she does not have the mental or emotional stamina to cope with the thought. She tells herself that she will do it tomorrow, but tomorrow never comes and before she knows it she just zoned out and watched three movies and ate a bag of chips and three bags of cookies.

And she wants me to say that we are making progress, that she is getting better, and that I believe she will someday be happy, go back to work and be whole again. And I talk about her changes and all the work she has done and how hard she is trying, but she is hearing background noises that make her hate her body, her face, her friends, her family. I know she is straining to hear me, but she is so far down the hole I find myself shouting and she can't reach my out stretched hand.

ABSTRACT

She sits in her seat at the art table,
Saying that she will do whatever I decide today because she doesn't care.
She carefully picks up her brush and starts painting big lush red strokes of thick paint and tells me about living in Saskatoon with her mom and learning to jack cars and steal food when she was ten.
Drug runners hid in her bedroom at night and she fell asleep watching the shadows of men crawl in and out of the windows on their nightly rounds.
She is having fun now using yellow, green and mixing everything together with no agenda or directions,
just fooling around in the paint.
She is liking the patterns that are forming on the canvas as she tells me about her mom's drug addiction and the night that Social Workers knocked on the door because a mean Aunt phoned and reported them.
She is making circles of swirling colour adding yellow and orange.
The orange hits a nerve and she pours it straight out of the bottle into the canvas craving more and more of it.
Then the car ride to a new foster home and how scared she and her brothers were and how badly they were treated not knowing that they could tell the Social Worker that the couple was starving them and hitting them when they misbehaved.
Now black outlines around the circles of mixed colours and she is thinking of adding sparkles. After that first foster home, it was a blur of moves.
She thinks maybe ten or more because she had an anger problem and kicked holes in the walls and broke windows.
At first they kept them together, then the three of them were too much to handle so they were separated.
She looks at her hands covered in paint and lifts her sleeve to show me the marks that still grace her arm where one of her fathers burned holes in her arm when she misbehaved.

CHAPTER 4

She washes the brush, pushes back her chair and says she likes it and is going to hang it on her wall.

And I tell her it is abstract art, free, open, full of wild chaotic energy, kind of like how her life has been.

And we both know that in this space, she can paint her way out.

MAKING THE DARKNESS GO AWAY

I worked with a little girl diagnosed with childhood depression.

I was supposed to make her happy, sociable, and likeable, you know, 'fix her'.

People jokingly say to me, "fix me," but I know they are serious. They want some quick Oprah program: The magic cure, answer, word.

When she came to see me, we made beads, and prisms, and hanging things for the window in the therapy room.

I sat contentedly with her in her quiet, sad, soft place of darkness and with our hands we made shiny things that reflected the light coming through the window.

Holding the place of her sadness, we spent a lot of silent time, months really, staring at the light shining through the hanging beads.

After a while, she asked her teacher to come see what we had made for the window, and then she brought in some of the kids from her class.

The principal and her teacher saw this as proof that she was coming out of her depression.

She was acting happy, more sociable, and likable. She was smiling.
Somehow, light had broken through her darkness and she was 'fixed.'

SHE IS GOOD AT DRAWING FACES

She is good at drawing faces,

Finding just the right curvature in the eye brow,

A good eye for detailing lips,

Knowing how to erase imperfections in the eyes,

Giving the right amount of shadow in the bridge of the nose.

She knows how to use the smudge stick to blend the lines and edges to create the right amount of softness.

She likes to use the pens and pencils,

Kept in a special wooden box,

The one I don't get out for everyone.

I explain how a lighter touch is better, how she can always go back in and darken any areas that need it,

How drawing faces needs practice, and how she has a talent for it.

She is not lured by colour or called to dip her paintbrush into baths of yellow or red.

For her, the magic lay in black and white and shades of grey,

leaving colour for someone else.

And when she comes before I get out the drawing materials,

She amuses herself by projecting lines against the white table,

Creating the forms that will fill the blank paper,

Practicing the skills of making her faces come alive.

SOMETIMES IT'S THE ART THAT NEEDS HEALING

"Why go over the past? How is this helpful?"
As she drew herself at 5 years old.
"These things are done; finished. This little girl who I am drawing is dead,"
As she marks a black X on the face.
It was a stick figure, a pencil drawing of herself
As a little girl staring out the window, crying.

I wanted to grab the drawing and hold it in my arms.
Like the time I saw a woman in a store
Repeatedly hitting her small daughter
Who was hiding under a clothing rack.
I tried to call security, but no one came.
And when he did, he looked at me like I had lost my mind.

I wanted to explain the power of voodoo
And making marks on images,
But I really don't know about voodoo.
But I do know about the power of images,
And I couldn't think of words to explain
The horror and hurt I felt.

She sat staring at the drawing.
"I am done now," meaning she wasn't coming back.

CHAPTER 4

For her, therapy would not help heal,
Or alter the past, present, or future.

Then I remembered a small boy I once worked with
Who had witnessed a murder and was fast becoming gang material.
But in one therapy session he softened
And drew himself as a flower.
He made me promise never to tell anyone
That, really, on the inside,
He was a flower: a beautiful yellow, with pink tips.

She got ready to go, collected her coat, and said,
"You can keep that picture. You seem to like it."
With tears in my eyes, I thanked her,
Saying I would look after it, and I placed it in my secret file
Of drawings by tough little boys who are flowers.

HOMEWARD BOUND

"I was 30 years on the farm and hated every minute" mother said, as she fed her children despair.

I thought, that the day I started to not like who and where I was, I was sure I would hate to do that all my life.

I was listening to Ken Wilber giving a talk and someone asked him if there were examples of women who arrived in the same place of enlightenment as had the men who spent years staring at walls. Ken talked about the women throughout history who attained pure consciousness *satori* by loving until it hurt. Men often transcend through the ego: meditating, releasing the ego mind. Women often transcend through doing, releasing the ego body. He talked of mystic nuns who sucked the wounds of lepers, emulating spirit, or pure consciousness through duty, actions, working with the sick, poor, hungry.

I never thought of my mother's dark illness as a doorway to *satori*.
I always thought, with regret that it was one door that I haven't been able to kneel in front of.

Now I understand that I walked through that doorway a long time ago and have never looked back.

OLD BELIEFS

I keep them close to me, so at night I can review them to see if I am still that same person, even if I hated her, she said.

Hmm, I replied listening to my client who was trying to close a particular chapter of her life.

I have a habit of needing to air out these short verses of grief and folded up memories of injuries so that don't I forget and stumble over them when I am not looking.

Hmm, I replied.
Because no matter how much positive thinking I do,
I still feel that I can't talk to him or tell him how I feel,
Even if I am trying to pretend that I can do this.

LIGHTING CANDLES

I remember your particular way of taking any life event and twisting and turning it into something lethal and dangerous,
The art you made, always sad, dark,
Your unique way of shedding gloom and darkness into every conversation.

I started lighting candles for you,
Nothing compared to your thick waves of despair and unhappiness.
But, still, a bubble of hope, a flicker of light.
Me praying that some warmth creeps in,
To mingle with your furious desire to stay in pain and darkness.

TEENAGERS

Dipping into forest green,
She paints scented fruits
Which, she tells me,
Live in hotels downtown.

Now she paints the sky blue,
Adds swirling clouds of birds that vanish.
She tells me how she hates her stepmother,
As some clouds vanish, now repainted
An orangy-yellow sun.

Which turns into a rose-yellow sun in a pale sky.
She hates her boyfriend and thinks he's really depressed,
Adding mist among the tree-boughs,
Dipping her brush into the white,
Then mixing it with grey.

Her best friend is probably pregnant, and her father
Will kill her. She thinks she may add a young beech tree

CHAPTER 4

On the edge of the forest,
But is not sure yet about the colour.

She wonders about creating some red deer
High on the mountain,
As she dips her brush into the mix of yellow, green, brown for the pine trees.
And, she got so wasted last Friday.
She didn't mean to, but her friend showed up
With all this alcohol,
So they went to the beach; the moon was so bright.

Now flowers appear, and she tells me she's skipping class,
She may fail two subjects, and she sleeps in class when she does show up.
She is painting rain, blue grey, then stops for a while
And we have tea.
She thanks me for not giving advice like everyone else and tells me
I'm the only one who just listens.
And I bite down hard on my therapist tongue.

THE RESISTANT THERAPIST

We who have the degrees, taken the workshops, learned the techniques
Are tired
Of your complaining, resistance, unwillingness to
Change, heal, get past, get over, get on with it.

Tired, of your endless excuses, disbelief, lack of resilience,
The imaginary symptoms, the reasons why
You stay curled up in bed with self-hatred, lack of confidence,
Fears and shame.

We are frustrated with the inconvenient positions you assume,
Your emaciation and trauma.
Frustrated with your complexity, conditions, history of layers of hurt.
The endless retraumatization, the need to revisit
The scenes of the crimes that keep
You suffering, bleeding, torn open.

We are unable to stay with your suffering:
The blank stares, the haloes of hopelessness,
Words of helplessness,
Physical limitations, lack of endurance, and the positioning of weakness.

All this offends our cherished sense that therapy works:
Things change, people get better, something can be done.
The right mantra, positive thinking, emotional release, cathartic moments;

All is better in the here-and-now.
There is a framework, goals, steps to follow, and ways
To eliminate your poverty, your hunger, your pain, your shame,
Your sorrow, your loss.

For we have neither the stamina, the persistence,
Nor the ability to go on listening.
We no longer believe in you, trust you, or want to pay
The cost of sitting here with you
Week after week.

We have suffered enough and are not getting better.
In fact we are getting worse. We have to let you go.

MENDING

You come here telling me that you don't want your loose ends mended.

Not because you lost all faith in the ability to start over or deal with one more disappointment.

But because you are not sure what shape you want the newness to take, if we come to that.

And somehow I convince you to sit and dream any possible scenarios and maybes.

We only need one, a thread to go forward ...

WHAT THE PICTURE TELLS

They are sitting around the table – Mom, Dad, two foster children -
Drawing a family memory.

Each, head down, thinking, drawing, picking out something,
All different.

This is foreign for Dad to draw his feelings, the way he sees.
Foreign enough that he can say things this way that he never has said.

Mom, too, senses a freedom, a difference in not getting through,
Of not being seen or heard by him.

And though the children start out timid, they can't help being truthful,
In their pictures.

And now that the words have stopped, I am thankful for all that we say.

CHAPTER 5

ART THERAPY AND AUTISM

Autism is a general term used to describe a complex group of neuro-developmental issues, known as Pervasive Developmental Disorders (PDD). It alters the brain and the nervous system. Autism affects language, social functioning, can interfere with sensory perception, and other learning and medical problems. The poem *Are You Human* is about a young boy who only had access to a hand full of words, which he repeated over and over. He loved exploring the world visually and tactilely. Art therapy is beneficial to children with autism spectrum disorders (ASD) due to their intense sensory needs. It offers visual and tactile self-stimulation and is visual, concrete, and hands-on.

The children I work with who live with this disorder have a variety of strengths, gifts, and creative abilities. We paint, draw, put on puppet shows, read and engage in many creative and fun activities. Art making helps develop fine motor control, stimulates right-hemisphere functioning, imagination and abstract thinking deficits, and promotes sensory integration. The poem *Is that all she does, just play?* explores the benefit of using Play Therapy with a child who does not use language as her primary way to express herself.

Art gives children, teens, and adults the opportunity to express powerful emotions. The process of making art, as well as the finished artwork, facilitates discussion about some of the issues they may be facing. Children can often say more in pictures than they can verbally articulate. The poem *Secret Bridges* demonstrates the use of sand tray in Play Therapy to give children a tactile tool to explore thoughts and feelings. In art making, they can represent a thought or feeling through an image, making it more tangible with a permanent record of their experiences.

The Same as Last Week Only Different and *She Thinks She is Sonic the Hedgehog* expresses how some autistic individuals have forms of repetitive behaviour. In the first poem, the boy I am writing about loved dinosaurs and monsters and could spend hours focused on talking about or drawing them. Often children with autism are encouraged to change their compulsive behaviour as it is viewed as a resistance to change. I have found that most children if allowed to follow their preoccupation with a theme or image will on their own move into change. Being allowed to express an image repetitively through art or play often helps children find the closure or resolution that they are seeking through creating it.

Stereotypy is repetitive movement such as head rolling, hand flapping, or body rocking. Often this is an attempt on the child's part to self regulate and/or calm themselves. The girl I am working with in the poem *If Birds Can Fly, Why Oh Why, Oh Why Can't I?* used repetitive movements to calm herself and we found that she could translate these repetitive movements into dance movements and hand gestures for songs. The term under-responsitivity means that someone is not responsive to their environment and often bumps into things unaware of what is around them and over-responsivity means the opposite that they are hyper aware of their environment and suffer distress from loud noises, clothes that feel uncomfortable, smells and/or light. Getting her involved in music, story telling and painting helped her move more comfortably into interacting with her environment. As an artist, she was in control of the environment and she could move in my Art Therapy Studio in ways that helped her calm not over stimulate her nervous system.

Self injury is also a problem associated with autism. Some of the children I work with practice eye-poking, skin-picking, hand-biting and head-banging. These are attempts to stop pain, frustration, and/or fear. When children can't communicate verbally and have impaired social interaction, they need some kind of other behaviour to demonstrate their feelings when overwhelmed.

Doing art with children is always uplifting, fun, and natural. I have never found a child that I couldn't invite to be involved in some form of creative activity. Cooking, building, painting, puppet shows, reading, singing – as long as I can be open-minded and inventive enough, I eventually find something.

With children, therapy is in playing. Things get worked out in process. So, I have lots of processes. Attachment repair happens through creating positive relationships. Self-esteem grows through pride in becoming successful creative beings, and the children become healthier as they learn how to relax their bodies and mind.

SHE THINKS SHE IS SONIC THE HEDGEHOG

She actually has been many characters; Sonic was just one of them.
When she was him, she made hedgehog outfits in the Art Therapy Studio and repetitively drew his picture until she got it right.
This behaviour is considered a core indicator of autism.
Words like "has obessions, circumscribed interests, routines, rituals, preoccupations" are thrown around when the diagnosis is made.
She fits the check list, qualitative impairment in social interaction, qualitative impairment in communication, restricted, repetitive and stereotypy patterns of behaviour and interests. It goes on, inflexible routines, complex whole-body movements.
And I can't help wondering if that is why Art Therapy works so well for her and others, because the descriptions of illnesses out of the DSM so closely match the descriptions of how to be a successful artist.

ARE YOU HUMAN?

I knew a boy diagnosed with autism,
Who would ask, "Are you human?"

Hearing him ask with his blank, open expression,
Stopped me in my tracks.

Am I? Am I being human? Who am I?
What does it mean to be human?

IS THAT ALL SHE DOES, JUST PLAY?

A new Social Worker has taken over the case and she is not sure what Play Therapy is or how it could possibly help this kid with his over-diagnosed problems.

She asks him, "So what do you do with Karen?" and he says "Just play." She says, "Do you talk." And he says, "Yeah, why?" and she says, "about what?", and he says, "The game of course," thinking that she is stupid and wasting his time.

And I send her reports talking about the value of play therapy, all the social skills he is learning, conflict resolution he learns, and the relationship building that happens. How it helps repair disordered attachment and creates attunement. How it helps him self regulate and deal with overwhelming feelings. How he feels heard and cared for as we interact and play together.

But she mistrusts the word. Somehow it sounds anti-therapy, not clinical enough, too unstructured or maybe, too much fun. And I wonder what she thinks he needs? And I try to imagine him sitting in a cold clinical looking office across from an older man stoically asking him questions about his feelings.

I watched him form trust, patience and empathy because he looks forward to 'just playing' with me. And I imagine her sitting in her office filling out progress reports and shuffling important papers thinking that this is serious business and that somehow I am fooling her into thinking that Play Therapy is somehow valid and useful.

And I remember the first time this violent, silently angry kid labeled with Asperger's actually shared with me and gave me an army man that he felt would match my team because he had taken all the good ones for himself and I wondered how I could explain to her that that was when I knew that all the weeks of hard play were paying off.

SECRET BRIDGES

Every child I see in art therapy is a work of art,
sometimes with a secret bridge or a road that digs underneath.

Mary has a tunnel.

CHAPTER 5

I don't know where it goes.
She doesn't either, but keeps searching
Through hollow stories with tragic endings
That make me want to cry out
"Let me fill in the flatness."
But she doesn't seem to notice.

Some have little parks.

Ronald has a park.
I always hope it will be beautiful.
It starts out with so much enthusiasm,
But never arrives anywhere that I can recognize,
Even though I try hard to see.

Some have floating islands.

Joe has islands with bridges and buried treasure
Without stories or characters.
I try to tell the missing story,
But he doesn't know the words.
Stories do not live in these islands or on these bridges.

These are not landmarks I know.

What are the lines, shapes, and colours I can't see?
Teach me this language.

THE SAME AS LAST WEEK, ONLY DIFFERENT

His Dad drops him off.

He starts quietly, checking the room,
Pacing, seeing if I have the right pencils,
Then if these are sharp.

Then he starts his story.
It's the same as last week, only different.
Always about monsters,
His stories explain which are dangerous
Which want to save the world.
He talks. I ask questions,
Not too many,
He doesn't like too many questions.

He draws new scenes,
Sometimes, the same scenes newly.

I draw with him.
Sometimes he walks as he talks.
Sometimes he sharpens the pencils,
Straightens the paper pile.

Then his story deepens, and
We touch a flow
Out into a field beyond autism, therapist/client, listener/talker
Into a connection I can't explain.
I want to wrap my arms around this place
Where there is no effort, no difference.

There is room in the world for this place, too.
It's the same as last week, only different.

A FREE DAY

You are quiet today.
This morning at school you must have not had too much noise or too many lights or too many smells to push you into that tight small place you often retreat to.
On this rare day, when you don't feel bombarded by sensory input that overwhelms and over loads until you are drowning in it all,
Your brain is ready to let you draw those pictures that you love.
And I wish everyday could be like this for you, free from the frenetic energy that builds in you until you almost burst because you process and understand differently.
And free from meltdowns because your sensory system just can't take it anymore.
And free from the mental overload that can happen without you knowing it until it is too late.
Today is one of those free days.
You don't need to pace, or cry, or get angry because you can't describe the feelings or frustration.
Today you are not going to hit yourself because of the self-hate, sadness, or desperation of having thoughts that will not stop.
Today there is no storm, only sitting quietly, drawing, talking a little and sipping tea.
Today is a free day.

IF BIRDS CAN FLY, WHY OH WHY, OH WHY CAN'T I?

I was thinking of a girl I work with, autistic, brain injured, who suffers from PTSD. Somehow we got talking about the Wizard of Oz. I think she saw my

CHAPTER 5

CD on the counter, I don't really know. Anyway, she saw the movie once or twice, but her support worker said she never really sat down and watched it. But when I played the CD, she knew most of the words. How could that be? Amazing!

She wanted to look at all the pictures, make Dorothy's shoes, create a wand, sing and dance to the music. For an hour in my art therapy studio, we sing 'follow the yellow brick road', make ruby red slippers, and laugh at the cowardly lion; we are home in the story.

This is a girl who stares blankly when I suggest anything, cannot sit still for more than a minute, can be violent, incommunicable. I am caught up in where this could go: We could work on the lack the characters feel they lack, to work with her sense of lack. We could take this tale of the hero's journey and make it hers.

We could write, do art. She could follow her dream – just like Dorothy. We could work with the witch metaphor, talk about those who have hurt her, those who have helped. She could play Dorothy for the people in her group home.

We could take it on the road….

'Somewhere over the rainbow
Skies are blue
And the dream that you dare to dream
Really does come true.'

Finally, I call myself home.
Come home, come home wherever you are!
I remember it's her story; her passion - this girl who
Seldom talks, is unresponsive to perform the magic she needs, she feels.

This is enough.
This is enough.

CHAPTER 6

ART THERAPY AND ADDICTION

As art therapists, we bring our own paradigms to the work. In working with clients who struggle with addiction, I combine Art and Play Therapy, Alcoholics Anonymous, Harm Reduction, the Trans-theoretical Model of Change, Mindfulness Practice, Somatic Experiencing, and Focusing.

The creative process itself is healing and, when combined with other paradigms, becomes a powerful tool in helping to heal addictions. Making art can be a way to relax, to change focus and mood. Clients can make art when feeling urges or restless. They can review their art to see how far they have come in their recovery. Making art in therapy can lead to a hobby – candle making, painting or working with clay. There is always something to pick up, to focus on, which can help the client move into a new lifestyle, to feel a creative, not a chemical high.

The appeal of art therapy in recovery work is that art can bypass the conscious defences and enliven treatment. Creativity is open-ended, dynamic, in direct contrast to a rigid, self-perpetuating, addictive activity. Creating helps integrate the right and left hemispheres of the brain, increases self-awareness, and allows access to nonverbal communication.

Creating helps clients focus on their islands of competence. Getting into art can help people become more resilient, providing physical and psychological stabilization. There is no right or wrong way to create art. Each person has their own individual expression: It is something everyone can do that moves people towards health.

The following poems focus on the complex twists and turns of addiction work. It is hard work helping someone face and heal addiction. The poem *As Long as It Takes* talks about the commitment that I witnessed that one First Nation band had to help another band heal. In a loving, accepting way they kept providing the opportunity for the others to join their healing circle.

The Right To Cut is about self-harm. Many of my clients self-harm due to suffering from depression, anxiety disorders, substance abuse, eating disorders, post-traumatic stress disorder, and /or other reasons. For this client art making opened up a whole new area of her life. She became passionate about creating art. Cutting was her coping mechanism and it provided relief from overwhelming feelings about her childhood abuse. Expressing her past through art making and doing Focusing sessions helped her move away from the need to cut.

The poem *Staying in the Trenches* is about a couple that were addicted to drugs and each other. Doing Art Therapy gave them a different perspective and way to

CHAPTER 6

communicate about their problems. Instead of repeating the same tired conversations they could view themselves and their relationship freshly through creating art images.

When I work with families, the focus is using art to 'see' family truths and views. The way families think, feel, and make sense of their experience becomes visual as they sit at my table and draw feelings, events, and imagined futures. Families do group collages stating wants, needs, and strengths. They can also paint individually, identifying resources, material support, advocacy, and companionship. When they make art, they and I can see everyone's point of view, and who is playing what role in the family. Art is a safe way to 'talk about' family secrets, money issues, and debt. It can be a safe way to be honest and talk about problems that may be hard to talk about. This helps counter family denial. Creating together helps build trust and cooperation.

A Difficult Bridge to Cross is a poem that I wrote in response to feeling frustrated by the pressure the family was putting on my client to change. After years of drinking and addiction, my client was starting the long journey to finding a healthy lifestyle. She loved painting. It gave her a calm, centred grounded feeling that nothing else could. It helped her slow down, stop worrying and for the first time in a long time, feel joy. Her self-esteem and self-confidence were slowly returning. She was starting to believe that if she could paint, maybe she could be good at other things too. It was empowering for her. Creating a piece of art gave her a feeling of accomplishment and pride, and conveyed to her the message that her creation mattered and helped her realize that she, too, was valuable. Creating something she felt good about gave her a feeling of optimism, ownership, and personal control. Connecting with her innate creative process helped her to reconnect with herself, enhancing self-esteem. When clients create art, hope is fostered.

AS LONG AS IT TAKES

I was on a reserve in northern British Columbia one Saturday night.
Most of the men, and some women, had been drinking
From a bowl that had aspirin, and alcohol,
And I don't remember what else, mixed in.
My friend, a white teacher hired by the Band,
Said it induced a 2 or 3 day crazy drunk.

It was warm that night as we walked around
Watching parents getting high and children playing with sticks.

Over in a corner a group of men were sitting in a circle.
They were from a neighbouring dry reserve,
Some quietly talking, some stirring a campfire.

I asked what they were doing.
A man said, "Waiting for the others to join us."

"How long will you wait?"
Stirring the fire, he said, "As long as it takes."

THE RIGHT TO CUT

My client and I are arguing about perspective.
She believes a therapist should always support the client's perspective.

"What if the therapist thinks the client's perspective is hurting her?"

"I can't support that."

"That's not support – that's abandonment."

"No! That's not wanting to stand by and watch you get hurt."

"I know what I need."

"So I am to support your need to hurt yourself?"

"If you can't support me in the way I need to be supported, you are not the right therapist for me."

"I am not capable of giving you support that leads to hurt."

"I knew you would abandon me; everyone does."

"It took you a long time to figure out how."

We both knew I lost.

REACHING THROUGH THE LAYERS

I work with women who, like my mother,
Make others into saints or sinners,
Usually both.

First, I am the Good Therapist,
God-like in my kindness, wisdom and compassion.

Then slowly, when I say the wrong word, show an unwanted expression, or turn left when it should have been right,

I fall into being the mother who never listened, the impatient sister who never waited, or the sadistic grandmother who never saw.

And it is hard to stay in the moment with "what is" when you are sitting with someone who is deeply embedded in "what was."

And it is harder still when "what was" has you playing the central role when you don't know the lines.

CHAPTER 6

I want to reach in through the layers of memories and invite her to simply sit with me.

Wondering if we can in this space, this moment, be safe from the ghosts of the past.

AFTERNOON THERAPY

It is not quite four o'clock and my stomach is empty,
Making growling noises and making me feel nauseous.
And I have two more clients before the end of the day.
And there is a soft blue glow coming from the lights in the craft room.
And outside I hear our dog Cyrus barking at unsuspecting passerbys.

You walk through the door, excited to be here,
Wanting to know what we are going to make today.
I notice the dark circles under your eyes, bleeding scabs on your arm,
Where you have been picking again.

I find myself impatient and wanting to lean in, talk about what matters,
Ask if you are cutting again, but this does not work like that.

You're antsy, wanting to make something, anything, loving working with your hands, settle on making jewellery as you get out the beads, chains and tools.

You start to relax, making the shift from your head where the squirming and stiffness lives into your hands where you are comfortable, smooth and flowing.

Your body no longer looks like it's about to crack at the seams…and the dullness is falling from your face.

And I notice, how little it takes for the softness to return.

STAYING IN THE TRENCHES

She crawls along through the stuck places,
Well dug into her relationship:
His lack of trust, her settling for someone she doesn't love.
We go over the same harsh words thrown back and forth,
That keep this marriage of pain alive.

I follow through a tired, heavy line of reasoning why she can't leave:
How here is better than nowhere,
At least he will not throw her out,
Though she thinks he's beginning to hate her.

I gently nudge her towards new ground, softer terrain,
But she holds tight to this landscape of disappointment and
Failed communication
Loving the hopelessness it wraps her in.

A METAPHOR

The therapist we saw, when our family was falling apart,
Said there's a metaphor for each step of life's journey,
Suggested naming the step might be helpful.

That was all she could offer – no solutions, ideas, words of wisdom –
As if finding a metaphor could change something
As traumatic, as painful, as what we were living through.

As if we were a family that she was reading about in a book
And I wondered if she got the idea from a workshop or a maybe she had read it somewhere.
Regardless, as I drifted off in my reverie I realized that at least she had taken my mind off my worries for a few minutes as I laughed at myself for actually thinking that therapy would not help.

WHAT A DANGEROUS BRIDGE TO CROSS

I know the money is running out and you want me to help change the deeply engraved patterns she has carefully dug for 58 years.
I know that she is difficult, resistant, suicidal, obsessive and confrontational.

I know all that.

I also know that here, in this room, where no one is lecturing her about her hoarding problem, she is not a hoarder.
And here where no one is cross examining her plans, she is not suicidal.
And when no one is telling her what to do, she is not confrontational.

I also know that my art therapy studio is not the world that she defends herself from.
I also know that to cross the bridge from here to there is tricky.
But maybe she is learning new steps and maybe some day when she leaves here, she will take the woman I *know* with her.

ON A GOOD DAY

I don't know what to tell you about first– the blank stare, the sad eyes, how he looked at me when I asked him if he knew that he was not going home, how

when we were sitting side by side making art I kept thinking that this can't be made right,
"How are you feeling?" I ask after delivering the news,
"I am O.K.," face looking pale and blank keeping out the dangerous words.
I could start anywhere, telling you about the broken social system that takes kids out of their homes and places them in worse ones, or I could explain attachment theory and how we all need our primary caregivers, or tell you about my worry that he will search for home the rest of his life.
The truth is right here, right now, for whatever reason we are in this room making art and on a good day I believe that we can heal.
But, on a day like today, I can't think of anything we could make together that would be strong enough to hold this pain.

EDGES OF KNOWING

You are so young and beautiful
And so bent on not making it.
And though I play at the edges of knowing of how to shift that,
I know that all I can really do is invite you to notice the light that flows into the studio window during the time that you are here, when your head is down drawing.
And believe that the small gestures that I show you, the special art supplies I buy, the way I beam when you enter the room, the genuine love I feel for you, helps, as you continue to build your universe in spite of your resistance.

IT WASN'T JUST

It wasn't just that he is always over drugged,
Although it was that, too.
It wasn't just the way he moves so slowly,
And takes so long to answer,
Although it was that, too.
It wasn't just that I love to see him laugh
As he beats me at Feeling Darts for the 100th time,
Although it was that, too.

It wasn't just that I wish I could do more,
Or get him to talk more or
Somehow be more awake or present,
Although it was that, too.
It wasn't just that I had too much coffee
And the winter snows had started and it was only October 22

Or that I needed to sleep
Because I was awake most of last night,
Or that I was hungry,
Although it was that, too.

It was about the whole system
And why he was here in the first place
And trying to do my best,
But feeling it was never enough.

It was about the feeling I had
When my daughter was little
And had done something unacceptable for the 100th time
And I wanted the whole world to change instead of her.
It was about the joy of guiding someone
To find a way into their voice, their creativity, their stories.
It was about wanting him to feel happiness, engagement,
Presence, and fulfillment.

But what if being fully present means
Knowing you will live in a group home forever,
That you will always have brain damage,
That you will always be on medication,
That no matter how many adjustments you make
Things will never be okay?

NOT ENOUGH

You write me emails reporting your latest struggles with your foster kids and I understand, being their therapist, that you, the foster mom, have to sound off to someone and I am supposed to believe that you are doing a super human job, fostering these problem children who have been abused and neglected by their drug addicted mom and deadbeat dad.

But, something is off here. It usually is when the foster children are First Nation and the foster mom is white, a certain tone, attitude that I am not quite in on, don't quite get. Maybe it is a subtle form of racism that I am not quick enough to pickup on because I want to believe that you love these kids, and because, in my naïve world, you are not supposed to feel this way.

So, I remind you of what a great job you are doing, and thank you for being there for these kids, not because I believe it, but because I am fighting for them and I know that at least in your home, even though you complain, you are not, I hope, abusing them, and we do not have enough healthy safe foster homes to move these children to.

CHAPTER 6

And I know that the system is broken and the cycle of abuse and neglect continues because we are not addressing the core of the problem and helping mothers mother and that we do not value children in this country, even though we pretend to.

And I tell myself that at least I am seeing these children for an hour a week and I fight to renew the contracts and that is something. And when I am really down I remind myself that when I was a child I had no one, not a grandmother, an Art Therapist or even a teacher telling me that I was special, or worthy of love.

And this is not enough.

CHAPTER 7

ART THERAPY AND GRIEF

Art therapy provides a safe way for people to 'talk' about fears, trauma, abuse, and secrets nonverbally, as in the poem *Dark Secrets*. Art making and therapeutic play is a type of nonverbal communication for children and adults who can't find the words in therapy. It is how children naturally explore, make sense of, and live in the world. The adults and children I work with love to create and look forward to their sessions, even though they know I may ask them about things into which they would rather not delve.

In *Building Candy Castles* and *Nests* I talk about the use of sand tray therapy. The sand tray is a multidimensional, experiential therapeutic tool. In a tray of dry and wet sand, clients build worlds. Using miniature, natural objects, dolls, cars, shells, dishes, and others things that represent all the bits and pieces of things that make up our everyday world, clients create scenes and pictures in the sand. These scenes by children and adults may reflect the feelings of home, work, the playground, the bedroom, a friend's house, or many other places in the client's life. There is not only the unmistakable feeling of playing in beach sand as a young child, but also of being a giant in a world of miniatures, where one can see the forest for having lifted out the trees. We can shape new images, recreate old memories, express feelings and, if need be, dismantle what we just made. We can connect and reconnect with imagery through diverse ways of playing within it. From this new perspective, we can plan new futures and revisit past experiences. Sometimes clients may re-experience preverbal states, use the sand to make cognitive decisions, and/or reconnect with a felt sense.

Sand tray therapy is a very open-ended, free, nonjudgmental way of working through/with feelings and ideas using figurines and objects. The therapist may be the witness to what happens for the client by holding space and being quiet, or may ask questions and guide, or be part of the creative process by also building alongside the client. Clients may communicate with their figures, or may write a story or poem to explain what is happening, or may remain silent. Sometimes clients talk about life issues. Clients may want to interpret what they have created or they may want to keep it in process and not talk about meaning. As in working with other mediums and techniques in art therapy, what happens is what needs to happen for each individual client.

Art therapy invites participation in a safe, supportive environment, where individual efforts at self-expression are reinforced to confirm their feelings are valid, their fears understood, and their needs legitimate. Visual images can work on many

CHAPTER 7

levels and can simultaneously express seemingly contradictory ideas and feelings. Art making allows one the comfort, support, and energy to go on with life. As a healing process, art making has been effective in promoting a sense of joy, peace, and relaxation. These important interactions between participants, art therapist, and the art process help move the participant from isolation and loneliness to connection and empowerment; from denial to acceptance; from loss of control and anxiety to relief; and from despair to hope.

The poems *Missing* and *The Sorrows of this Job* speak to the uncertainty of the future of many of the children and teens that past through my Art Therapy Studio. Many of the children and youth with whom I work have witnessed a death of a family member, experienced a death of a friend or have tried to commit suicide.

BUILDING CANDY CASTLES

In the sand tray, you are building the perfect place to live
That, for a 5-year-old, is made entirely of candy:
Ice-cream cones for houses,
Cookies for the stores, and the school of cake.

The girls are calling you fat
And the boys are punching you when you aren't looking,
And you, at the tender age of 5, are starting to understand
The layers of pain that get hidden in the soft pleasures
Of chocolate cookies and too much pop.

But here, with no one looking,
We can build lavish, overflowing, rich sugary walls
That satisfy no one, but have become your weight to bear,
And, somehow, here in this room with me,
We have to find our way out of this sticky,
Sweet illusion because already at 5 years old,
It is killing you.

As we work to build the city, the spell slowly breaks
And the echoes of loss that these creams and icings
Were to keep out, start bursting from the seams.
The walls collapse under the weight of a 5 year old
Accepting that she can't live with
The burden of a father dying of cancer and the feeling
That, somehow, it is all her fault.
This part of you that the power of the candy can no longer cover up,
Lays naked, exposed in the sand,
And, together, we will keep it alive.

THE MAGIC OF ART

I used to work with a little boy
Who thought we could make anything –
Magic swords, stones that talked,
Books that came alive at night.
And when he came for his sessions,
for an hour we could.

DARK SECRETS

The children I work with have dark secret gardens within, to hide.
A place to go away to,
When all seems hopeless, helpless, lost.
    Tears mostly of blood.

Sometimes it feels like it's my job to pry open when, really,
What I do is ask if I can sit down beside,
Be with, and hide there also in that place
Where we both could fall asleep forever.
    Where all seems quiet, dark and deep.

Nothing grows but shadows, painful memories fed by fear.
I look around thinking I may find a corner that could shelter
Or a small oasis, not yet discovered.
    Who knew that rocks could hug or
    Seedlings could grow out
      Of our chests?

Here in this place, fresh life springs out of painful, bloody cracks.

I used to garden when I lived on Pender Island. I had a beautiful 3-acre organic garden filled with flowers, herbs, and vegetables. I remember the day, while cutting a plant, it hit me how cruel this was – to grow things and later turn around and kill them. Shortly afterwards, we sold the farm and I have never really gardened since. Or is this my new garden – planting seeds, fertilizing, encouraging growth that later someone will cut down and destroy?

FRESH BEGINNING AFTER HER HUSBAND'S DEATH

A story starts with its own telling.
She says she appears to be doing well in the script,
Her part surprisingly free of self-doubt, self-blame.
But she can't help waiting for the next page –

CHAPTER 7

The longing for things to turn sour –
Because all this goodness hurts too much.

THE BOY WITH THE BEAUTIFUL EYES

When the boy with the beautiful eyes started talking,
I wanted to cry.
My heart fluttered at the sight of his sweet face and graceful fingers.
I remember a social worker telling me once that sooner or later there would be one child that I would not be able to say goodbye to, that I want to adopt him or her.
I admit that I sat there shaky and confused, not expecting the unreasonable tugging at my heart. So many of the children walked in and out of here, why him, why now?
And Cody, unaware of my startling dilemma, was playing as though my heart had not just been hijacked, and looked over with a smile, just for me.

THE MAGIC CLOTH

We went on a 3-hour picnic.
She reminded her foster mom for weeks ahead that
We had a 3-hour picnic scheduled.
Usually, she comes to see me for 1 hour,
But this time it would be for 3.
I bought a new cooler, all her favourite foods,
Packed my camera, prepared games for after dinner.

She was so excited; so was I!
We had never been together outside the therapy room.
We had our table set, food laid out, drinks,
When a family arrived and
Sat down at the picnic table next to us.

I knew it was coming, it always did.
"A cloth, you should have brought a cloth!"
As the mom spread out a clean, white table cloth.

I tried to defend my lack of planning
By pointing out how the wind
Blew up the edges of the cloth and
Rocks had to keep it down.
But, no matter.
I could not pull her – or
All my other children who live in foster homes –
Away from trying to figure out why
She was not at the picnic table with the white cloth.

I wish it could be that simple.
But is it really so different than
What I do as a therapist, a researcher, a writer?
Aren't we all looking for the magic cloth?

PRESENCE

She set you free,
By painting that wide-open field where you could
Work all day on your tractor.
I helped her pick the paint,
Prime the canvas.
She made sure the sun was hot,
The way you liked it
Before the accident.
She still visits the farm, with her son and husband,
But it's not the same. How could it be?
She has painted that, too:
Scenes of abandoned farm machinery, overgrown fields.

And then she started making boats.
I'm not sure why. But lots and lots of boats,
Woven with materials she finds in my studio.
Just the right shape, feel, and lines to stop her wounds from bleeding.
She wants to set them in the ocean,
Saying you had never seen it, up close.
In them are written messages,
Goodbye letters to you.

She was born and raised on the Prairie, with no-nonsense thinking,
Wanting none of my West Coast metaphors
About grieve boats,
The ocean, her unconscious suffering,
Or his journey to the other side.
She says, "This is not a poem, damn it!
It just feels good to make these and talk about Dad's death."
"Dad was no fool, I tell you. But,
He would never understand this art therapy stuff."

She remembers how he worked with his hands,
Carving for her when she was little,
As her fingers lead her to the right shapes and colours
That heal the wounds
Of a death that came too soon.

CHAPTER 7

And we both feel a sudden chill. Then a presence warms the room,
And watches us working at the table.

But on the Prairie, there's no need to talk about this.

NESTS

She only plays with rocks.
We arrange them, carry them in little bags,
Sometimes, count them.
Often, we place them in groups on the couch while we have tea.
She moves slowly, softly, laughingly.

She is here for grief counseling.
Her brother died; she is four.
They played together every day,
And now she has nightmares, can't eat, and
Won't talk about him.

Today we are placing the rocks in little nests.
We are filling the nests with feathers and shells.
I want to add beads, but she says
"That is silly!" and so I don't.

When we are done our nests,
Without beads, are eight.
We have them carefully lined up,
Sure that each one has an equal amount,
Snuggled in the sand.
Some with feathers, some with shells, but none with beads because
"That would be silly!" of course.

It is time for her to go.
I wonder how is this therapeutic?
How is this helpful?
In cleaning up, I see under the sand tray
A carefully placed little nest filled with beads.

Play heals what words can't express.

WANTING MOM

Slow. Discovery. Opening drawers in the studio. Finding a package of eyes
– Leads to wanting to make a gift for Mom.
– Leads to finding red material for lips.
– Leads to looking for white paper, glue, and crayons.

Slow. Discovery. Lining things up on the table. Starting with the paper
– Leads to drawing a picture of herself and Mom.
– Leads to talking of how she still doesn't know why she can't live With Mom, why she is in a foster home.
– Leads to her saying she thinks Mom doesn't want her anymore,
How she can't sleep at night, how she has nightmares, and how she
Wishes she could disappear and die.

Slow. Discovery. Looking for a box to put the picture in. The perfect box
– Leads to both of us saying how wonderful the picture is.
– Leads us to wrapping it with bright ribbon and stickers.
– Leads her to talking of how much Mom will love it at her next
Home visit. She will love it so much that it will make everything OK. Maybe she can go back home, and Things will be back to normal.

Slow. Discovery. How do I explain to a 5-year-old that the world doesn't work that way?
– Leads to me wanting to make everything all right.
– Leads to me wanting to pretend that this time the world will work
That way – the picture will change things, her mom will stop using;
Everything will be okay.
– Leads to me to falling on my knees in despair.

A MAKE OVER

I am cleaning the worktable where children have been making Christmas angels and painting on small cards.
I think of the decades of people making things and children creating,
Something new for the first time.
Suddenly, I notice that it feels far too lonely in this room where I, alone,
Struggle with how to make things better, different, or just to make things.

The making of things that my Mother, Grandmother, Aunts, and sisters
All did: making to make "of," to make "as if," to make "anew."
Now, in my art therapy studio, a boy just left, and I wonder
What he makes of coming here for art therapy?
His past 13 years are full of sadness, loss, and sorrow.
Will he make it?

We sewed a magic bag to wrap around,
To help calm him down when stressed.
He made a friendship bracelet for his girlfriend.
He likes to make things; he's good at it.
Fast, smart, wise fingers.
He looks through the cabinets of the sewing machine, given by a friend,

CHAPTER 7

And finds her mother's ribbons, bobbins, threads:
The leftovers bits of making things.

I want to make it better or at least okay.
I help him cut, sew, add rice for the bag.
This making together, will it make a difference?
When we play darts and one lands on the floor,
Joe says. "that's a makeover!"
Can it be as simple as that?
Are we making over?
The years when no one watched, marvelled at his making?
Are we making over?
The years when life was violent, unpredictable?
Are we making over?
The years when he was alone, hungry, hurt?
Are we making over?
Are we making over?

THE SORROW OF THIS JOB

A new client, First Nations, 13, troubled, beautiful, talented,
Talks a lot, then sometimes not at all.
Depends on her mood, as with most 13 year olds,
Only most 13 years olds were not raped, drugged, and tortured.

She misses her Dad, her Grandmother who raised her,
But not the men who raped her.

I want to tell you about
How beautiful, strong her profile is
In telling me she wants to be a journalist.
And how she can paint and draw.

I don't want to tell you
I have felt her desperateness before,
I know the cutting rawness of this feeling.
I wish despair was not wrapped around her story
That hope would break through any minute.
But I don't see it entering the room and
There's an unmistakable whisper of something else.

MISSING

I have been thinking about a client who has gone missing.

Many teens I see from group homes go missing all the time; AWAL they call it.

They usually run to North Central, a place where lots of relatives, boy friends, ex parents live and the cops sooner or later find them – it is a small city.

And then I remember my daughter, two years old, red boots on and a hiking stick saying good-bye when we lived on Saltspring Island – walking down the middle of the road – neither of us thinking that she would really go.

But that was an innocent leaving – full of fantasy adventurous play and no risks – not the kind reserved for my clients who walk blindly into the kind of hell we reserve for native girls and never want our white children to know about.

Right now she could be struggling as a stranger is trying to
stuff her body into a tight hole that has no air.

I watch for her name in the paper, ask her friends if they have heard anything, ask her Social Worker if she has any news, but it seems like everyone wants to forget.

Maybe it is a Canadian tradition to pretend we didn't see another native girl who didn't wave good-bye.

MY TEACHER

Sitting together in that small room
At the Art Therapy School on Lee Ave.,
I was a student and you, my first practicum client.
Practicum – to practice with – being new at this therapy stuff.

Facing each other, in a closet really,
Closing out the world,
We thought, for some small reason,
For an hour we were safe.

Sitting together in that small room
You told me of the 20 plus electrical shocks,
In the early 60s, in an asylum in Toronto.
How it confused your thoughts, but didn't ease
The paranoia, the fear, the memories
Of your Father's beatings, his raping you
Because your Mother left him for another.

This is, in another space.
It is in the thought that we created for ourselves
Out of all the pieces:
This place to make anew.

CHAPTER 7

Sitting together in that small room,
You rolled wax candles.
I think you loved the waxy feel.
Mostly, we made collages.
You picked out pictures from magazines
Of things that you remembered.

With each picture, the cutting out,
And slowly pasting down,
Came stories of your children,
The jobs you had, the cities you had lived in.
I listened, asked questions, and forgot we only had one hour.

Within a single thing, a single story,
Wrapped tightly round us,
A warmth, a light,
Slowly grew against the dark.

Sitting together in that small room,
I learned you suffered from bipolar
And that horrid things had happened, mostly in those hospitals.

But you, talented with your hands,
Had raced cars, built a house with your first husband,
Learned to weave, to sew,
Travelled by yourself through the desert.

Here, now, we forget the outside world.
We feel the pull of the images,
As we weave new knowings,
That light our way.

Sitting together in that small room,
I learned about your struggle to kill yourself.
The voices in your head were sometimes quiet,
But other times they screamed day and night.
They had started again, telling you to cut your wrists.

We light the candles, telling stories in the dark,
Knowing that the imagination is fighting hard
To keep us hidden here.

Sitting together in that small room,
We finally ran out of time. And,
Because I was young,
Because I was to be the therapist,
Because I didn't know then what I know now,

I didn't know what you meant
When you said that you felt human
Because I *saw* you.
I should have thanked you for this teaching.

Out of this same light,
Lit by feeding stories into,
We make a dwelling in this space,
Where being seen together was enough.

THE STORIES NOT TOLD

Sometimes I don't tell you,
Because I'm not sure how.
Sometimes it's because,
The words are new – too close, too fresh. I'm not sure they could stand being said out loud

Sometimes it's because
The words include the lives of others
Who cannot defend, speak for themselves,
And may not want to be trapped into my made-up meanings.

Sometimes it's because
I don't know if these words are necessary –
They may be too loose, too unorganized, scattered.
Sometimes it's because
I can't find the line between disclosure and discretion.

Sometimes it's because
The story needs to percolate,
To shape into something that's tellable.
Sometimes it's because
I know that the stories I tell
Shape me and I'm not sure yet,
How I want my story shaped.

Sometimes as I am building, deepening my own story,
I get lost and must return to the beginning,
Re-envision the ending,
Before I can say more
About the present.

Sometimes as I am moving
In and out of stories,

CHAPTER 7

I forget the stories that need to be told and
Those to keep tight, close.

Sometimes I remember
To trust the stories,
Letting them decide.

SUPER HERO

I am seeing you as a little super hero,

Riding your bike with your baby sister on the back,

All the way to your neighbour so, they can phone 911

Because you can't find your mom's cell phone.

And after you made sure that your sister was safe,

You turned around and rode your bike back to your mom's

And held her head in your lap until the ambulance came.

And as you are telling me this, I see you as five going on 45 and I wonder how you fit in with the other kindergarten kids whose biggest problems are if they will get computer time when they get home.

And you worry that when your mom gets out of the psych ward, you won't be able to see her and you need to because you are the only one who can help her when the voices tell her to stab herself.

And some days I don't know what to do, think or feel, but you are a super hero. That I know for sure.

CHAPTER 8

ART THERAPY GROUPS AND HONOURING THE MOTHER

For years I facilitated a group called 'Honouring the Mother' for women who want to explore their image and the issues of motherhood with other women – issues such as isolation, self-esteem, self-talk, self-care, and community. The women in this group loved making art and not having to cleanup. They got to be with other women without their children interrupting them and talk, play and create art. My favourite part was when they shared their stories and art process with the group – stories of loss, heartache, love, and wonder. The poem *Don't Talk, Just Listen* speaks of the need to be listened to in a compassionate, nonjudgmental way. Story is the paramount way to understand the world and our experiences. The stories in this group were sometimes heart breaking as in *Being a Mother* and sometimes funny but they bound us together as we struggled with big and little life issues. Story is how we think, make sense of experience, and cultivate our imagination. Through storytelling, artistic responses, and experimentation, we can explore and develop our imaginations and creative abilities in a safe, fun, and creative environment.

Group members did many different art activities and then shared in the group how the art experience was for them. Some of the projects were reinventing aprons to make a statement about Mothering, creating casts of their hands to talk about the work, play and touch that Mothering invites, making Mandalas, and clay creations showing their family systems. The poems *Making Aprons* and *Hands* talk about the art experience. I would often invite the women to work in collage so they could experience the spontaneous, surprising results that collage can provide.

This art therapy group helped create community and build friendships. Some of the women who attended my groups still meet. The following poems are glimpses into some of their stories.

BEING A MOTHER

For 7 years I have worked with a woman
Whose husband died of Huntington's disease and
Both her children, now in their 20s, have the same disease.

Her daughter is in-and-out of the hospital, terminally ill;
Her son in university is okay, for now,
But wrestles with depression.

CHAPTER 8

Every day she checks him for signs of the disease.

In my client's visits, she is hopeless, suicidal, and depressed.
Each week, I somehow help her to release some anxiety, find some peace,
And/or moments of conscious awareness out of this drama.
The Health and Legal systems have let her down,
And, she has no money.

There is no therapeutic, social, medical, or emotional cure.
But, somehow, she is staying strong enough to watch her children die.

Some things are worse than death.

HEDGEROW TEACHER

As a child, I did not really think of Mother as a real person. She suffered from mental illness and my family ignored most of her behaviour, pretending things were different, finding ways to normalize an abnormal situation. She was not 'home' so to speak, so could not provide one for her family. I spent secret hours writing poems I kept in a tin box in the rock fence up the lane. I covertly taught songs I liked to rows of snowmen and held private summer art classes for my dolls in the lilac bushes.

When I was older, I learned about Irish hedgerow teachers. I imagined them teaching in the bushes, as I did in the lilacs. They taught their students Gaelic and other subjects under secluded hedgerows during the struggle for Irish independence from the British. They were evicted, as was I, from their home.

The habit of hiding to learn and teach became embedded. I loved the lure of secret rituals, symbols, metaphors and looked under the surface for their meanings. I loved dark, secretive places and feel at home in their cave-like structures. The surface – the exposed, the obvious – was unsafe, it could twist and turn as my mother's moods and words. Setting up camp in a bush for an hour, a day, or a week, where love could be discovered in a book or a box of crayons was my home.

A BAD MOTHER

My client is talking about being a bad Mother.

You know … a Mother who saves her anger to throw that perfect remark,
Directly, deeply at the last person in the world she wants to hurt –

Her daughter.
But there it is. There is no taking it back, making it better.
It is embedded so far that it's now part of her daughter's dark, foul self.

The last thing she wanted was to repeat her own darkened childhood,
Where her Mother's rage streamed into her upturned face,

And ripped through her attempts at a happy childhood.

My client is talking about her Mother, you know, the kind of Mother who
Poisons all the things her children could have been,
A Mother who should have come with a large neon sign:
Do not believe what I say about you.

But there it is.

She has not forgotten or forgiven the bloodstains and the hurt.

It is embedded so far that she has no strength to pull it out
And fill it with clarity, kindness, or compassion.

The last thing she wanted was for her anger, again today to fall,

On her daughter.

And none of this, none of this matters as she sits and cries in my arms.

WHAT IS MY PROBLEM?

I always thought the problem was the complexity of it all.
My ongoing confusion, the contrary voices in my head,
The not knowing, the self-doubt.

I always thought that if I had a clear desire, goal, or sense of where
I was going,
Then things would unfold smoothly.
I have seen it happen:
Small things I wanted, coming without effort.
But when I retrace my steps,
I never can remember how it happened
Or what the magic formula was.

I always thought the problem was too much to balance.
My desires, the children's, my partner's all tangled up
So they had to compete.

I always thought that if I had a clear focus, intent, or plan of what
I wanted the future to look like,
Then things would unfold smoothly.
I have seen it happen:
Change manifested without pain.

CHAPTER 8

But when I try to figure out the next move,
You ask me to drive you somewhere;
You need help figuring out why no one likes to play with you; and
You want dinner.
In the midst of it all, a small part of me holds tight.

RESILIENCY: MISSING PIECES

When I was younger,
I always felt I was missing some inner strength, some part.
Instead of supporting myself, I would just collapse.

I was on the school track team, taking part in a meet in Verona.
I was in the lead, but coming around a corner,
I collapsed on the ground.
My track coach angrily asked why I gave up.

I couldn't answer; I just knew I didn't have it in me to finish.
I felt like something in me was broken or missing.
My brother told me I was the runt of the litter;
There wasn't enough left for me.
And, he was the one in the family who liked me.

AT 50

Needing to take stock, she says, about her selves.

Partly settled, partly in resolve, her multifaceted set of selves.

Old selves struggling with new selves.

Exactly how this happened and is happening she doesn't know.

Started with her daughter moving on, not needing her,

Started with vague dissatisfaction with work,

Started with a remark someone said that stuck in her brain.

"I never thought that things would go this far," she says sitting in my office.

I say, "Change is like that. Any piece of friction can attract it. We seem hardwired to move ahead."

"Yeah, exciting," she says, as she digs deeper into the chair.

DON'T TALK, JUST LISTEN

Something had happened, and I wanted to tell her.
I didn't want opinions, advice, or wise comments.
I just wanted to be listened to.

I wanted the messy, unresolved feelings heard,
Not tidied up, rearranged, neatly packaged.
I wanted them received raw, chaotic, unattractive;
I wanted them loved as they were,
Not how they should, could, might be.

I wanted someone to meet me in this open wound.
I hoped I could do that for her.

MAKING APRONS

I bought aprons from a second hand store thinking that they would make a great art therapy exercise.

I would invite the women to remake them in any way that inspired them. It could turn into a political piece critiquing the traditional role of mothering, or portray the myths of Motherhood, or maybe a sentimental piece about their own mothering or a glimpse into how they were mothered.

They proved to be as diverse and interesting as I thought they would. One woman made hers into an apron for a motorcycle riding, rock and roll loving Mother, another showed the things a woman loved doing with her children in each season, another had her apron pockets filled with symbolic items that showed the joys and sorrows of mothering.

But my favourite was a heavily pocketed apron filled with small surprises and little toys. The maker of the apron was a difficult woman often opinionated, overpowering, and overbearing. And, she loved her daughter and told sweet beautiful stories about their relationship as she pulled the items out of the pockets one by one.

But in groups, as in life, we tend to see our family members in others and this woman soon became the oppressive Mother that many knew too well. And I watched these women brace against her sharp edges and quick wit knowing how to slip and slide around a Mother that you could never be sure of.

And I marvelled at their power of making art together. How here in this small intimate gathering of random mothers drawn to a therapy group that promised art, stories, tea and companionship, even here, in this safe clearing, good and

CHAPTER 8

evil forces entered. And we always have a choice of re-creating our pain or reinventing a fresh story. Even through the pockets of an apron.

HANDS

We are at the Monday night "Mothering Group" and tonight we are making hand casts.

Wet rolls of plaster stretched over the fingers, fitted 'just so' over the tips of each finger.

We sip tea as the finished casts dry and the women start talking about their hands. Deep memories and birth stories have been triggered, maybe the plaster bandages reminded them of sterile hospital rooms or maybe it was the tender attention of their art partners as they gently wrapped the fingers, wanting to get it right.

Out pouring of stories of hands that were not quick enough to catch falling babies from change tables, or fast enough to pull back a small inquisitive finger from a hot burner, or intuitive enough to know when a toddler was going to dart in front of a car.

Hands that had not comforted enough night fears, taught enough life skills, or wiped away enough tears.

But now the casts were dry, so teacups were rinsed and paint brushes picked up. And maybe it is the gift of the flow of colours or the release of the stories, but somehow the hands that before where full of lack and regret started to take on a strength and resiliency. And maybe it is just that the creative process knows how to use personal doubt and regret to conjure up new colours and symbols. Or the grace of silent forgiveness when you can tell your dark secrets to a room full of women and not one sees you less than courageous.

CHAPTER 9

ART THERAPY GROUPS AND MAKING PEACE WITH YOUR BODY

For years I have facilitated an art therapy group called 'Making Peace with Your Body,' a group for women who want to explore body image, eating, and issues with food with other women. In this group, women explore their relationship to, perception of, and feelings about their bodies. Body image is a complex subject for women. We grow up with a limited, stereotypical perception of an acceptable female body image as portrayed in poems *But I Am Fat ...* and *Paper Dolls*.

Beginning in infancy and early childhood, traumas accumulate in the body. All traumas involve some level of dissociation from the body as I talk about in *Body Blocked*, and the degree of dissociation reflects the intensity of the trauma. Therapy intends to create association with the disconnected parts of the self. The autonomic nervous system can learn to self-regulate again through 'repairs' that transform the activation of the system. These repairs can happen through art therapy, visualizations, somatic experiencing, EMDR, focusing, and other right-brain therapy techniques.

In *Body Maps* and *Making Peace* I talk about how creating body outlines, body plasters, and masks is a creative, deeply effective way for women to reflect on and 'see' their bodies in a different light. In this art therapy group, we use meditation, focusing, art therapy, and other tools to work with the interpersonal relationship that we have with our body.

Focused oriented art therapy is an integrated, somatic-centred approach used with art making. Focused oriented art making facilitates the ability to stay present with inner bodily sensations that result from engaging the senses. This awareness or connection to bodily sensations and feelings is expressed through art. This process enables a deeper body/mind connection and allows a richer integration of experiences in resolving traumatic or overwhelming events.

Somatic psychology, EMDR, art therapy, and focusing are all part of the context. Somatic psychology links the neurophysiology and psychology to the wisdom of the body as it relates to trauma resolution and the inherent stress of daily living. Through the art process, as described in the poem *Body Maps*, one can explore and expand on the authentic creative imagery that comes from the body work. Through body awareness and creating imagery, one can work towards transforming trauma.

It is a process of awareness, a natural process, but one that can also be learned. It is taking the time to sense in the body the 'whole way' that one feels, senses, and thinks about a situation in one's life. Getting a felt sense is getting a fresh feel of how something is in this moment. It is learning to stay, with interested curiosity, and to be

CHAPTER 9

with the felt sense, so one can hear what the body knows as one expresses it through making art images, playing, or working in the sand tray, as the poem *Making Peace* portrays. One is witnessing, being with, and forming a supportive interrelationship with one's self. In this nurturing relationship, all is welcomed, accepted, listened to, and respected. One is settling down with one's inner experience and getting to know it better. Deep inward listening can cause a release, a relief, and a 'letting go.'

BUT I AM FAT ...

I tell my client how amazing her last art show was.
She smiles, says she feels much better about herself and her work,
But adds, "I am still fat."

Years ago my partner, myself, and our daughter,
Who was 2 at the time, stayed overnight at another teacher's home.
She had organized a conference,
While continuing to teach her Grade 2 class and was
Hosting us and another family for the weekend.

I commented on what a wonderful job
She had done balancing school, the conference,
As well as making us feel so welcome in her home.

She took the compliment, smiled, and said,
"Now if I could only lose 10 pounds!"

PAPER DOLLS

We are in my therapy room at 1:00 on a Tuesday afternoon. My client is talking about people who she wants to be like: the confident, sleek, and accomplished. She remembers moving through life in a casual, carefree way, unburdened by traumatic memories and her recent gain in weight. In talking about her strong, thin trainer at the gym, she says, "I want to look like her." But, really, it's not about the look that she is after or even the way her trainer's body bends and moves so elegantly, effortlessly.

I remember playing with my Doris Day paper doll as a child. That doll was so thin, so free of pain, worry, and doubt. She had amazing clothes, perfect blond hair, and she always smiled. Life for her was easy and free of struggle. It seemed the paper was too thin to hold any hurt or pain or sorrow of lost loves or leading movie roles.
There's no therapeutic exercise that can flatten my client's aching body to the thinness of paper, but it can prevent her pulling out the scissors.

ART THERAPY GROUPS AND MAKING PEACE WITH YOUR BODY

SNOW WHITE

Standardized images of one-size–fits-all:
"Red as blood." State the size and shape of lips, hips, breasts.

"As white as snow." Young girls check themselves in mirrors.

For she was a thin little thing, but learning fast about self-hatred
The kind that bites down hard and spits out "shiny apples."

"And black as ebony." A recipe filled with poison.
She did not have three wishes standing on the scales and
Weighing into another's fantasy.

When under a spell, one can't stop sweeping and cleaning up
Till the dwarfs are all asleep.

YOU AND ME

What this means is that:
Just as we're opening up this shame, this deep hurt, this painful place
As we are newly being born,
There's always a chance of being bent the wrong way;
Of not coming out right.
Being pulled in confusing directions,
With so many sad conclusions,
So many dangerous memories,
So many words, images, emotions.

What this means is that:
Just as you struggle with birthing,
Gently opening,
With the hope of new beginnings
Where grace fills the wholeness,
Then a "midwife" with spread-open hands
Delivers safely what always was yours.

BODY MAPS

Twelve women, all with different degrees of hatred for their bodies
Hoping that this group can change all that,
Or at least point them in a new direction.

And tonight they are doing body maps,
Filling them in with resources or things that help them feel more grounded,
Connected to their bodies.

CHAPTER 9

And this session they are using images cut out of magazines, handmade papers, Chinese paper money, stencils, origami papers and whatever else they can find, In my paper boxes.

Heads down, chatting, laughing,
Some tears but mostly busy hands cutting and pasting.
Creating without too much thought of why.
And that beautiful group flow energy has happened as it does sometimes,
When inspiration overtakes doubt; ease replaces hesitation, and joy floods up,
And over fear.

YOU WERE PART OF THAT GROUP

You were part of the body image group.
Saw a sign advertising an Art Therapy group and you thought, 'why not'?
You, so talented, raw and beautiful,
You showed up to every session even though you never talked to any of the other women but me
And you showed me your artwork and invited me to hear your all girl band and you were so grateful, you said, to a have a place to come where the noise would stop.
We started each session with a short meditation and even though you had never meditated before, you said it felt like coming home; warm, familiar.
And I noticed the scars on your arms and legs, the black eyes, the signs of depression, after all I am a therapist I know what to look for and I said any time you wanted to talk after the group I would hang around.
But you always had to run off to band practice or a boy friend or a party.
And you asked me out for afternoon coffee and I explained that I worked all day and I told you if you ever wanted to see me in my Art Therapy Studio, you were welcome.
But you were not ready for that you said, you couldn't face your demons.
I said, any time just call. And I ran into you at a few down town art shows and you looked like you were doing 'okay'.
But I can't help thinking I could have done more.

BODY BLOCKED

You are talking about your body like it belongs to someone else,
A friend who has betrayed you and in disbelief, you walked away.
This has gone on for years, you and your body living separate lives.

And I am finding this harder to navigate than couples counselling because at least with most couples there is still a desire to work things out or they would not be here sitting in my office.

But you want me to somehow help you sever off what you have already dissociated from and therapy works to harmonize and integrate not disconnect and destroy.

So, we will start gently from the beginning and see what the attraction was before the love was lost.

MAKING PEACE

We are working in the Art Therapy studio on a mask.

You want it to portray your feelings about your relationship with your body. On the inside, you decide to show how you feel and think after you binge; heavy, tired, twisting pangs in your stomach, headaches and dark thoughts full of self hatred.

You say that the worst part is never having a normal relationship with food, never being able to just eat without all the thoughts and self criticism and fears. All this you pour into the mask through colours, lines, shapes and images and slowly you start breathing a bit deeper and talking a bit clearer.

You are now remembering your childhood and what it was like to feel at home in your body, jumping high and running fast. Food was not the enemy and life was not a struggle. You finish the inside with painting thick black horizontal bars to show how you feel imprisoned by the addiction of monitoring every single thing that goes in your mouth.

You flip the mask over and decide that you want to paint how you would imagine freedom would look, if you could be at peace in your body, if life was not a burden. And slowly you start painting yourself there, into that space. Breathing it in like a reunion with a long lost friend that has been quietly sitting and waiting to catch your eye.

CHAPTER 10

ART THERAPY GROUPS AND THE ARTFUL ARCHETYPAL JOURNEY

I have taught year-long archetypal groups for many years which I describe in *A Poem About the Archetypal Group*. Usually, we meet in groups of 8 to 10 women and talk about different archetypes and how they represent a part of us. We share stories, tea, and create art. In the poems *The Fool Archetype*, *We All Have The Right To Cast Spells*, and *Those Who Know and Remember* I talk about three different Archetypes and their meanings.

Archetypal stories are universal, enduring stories that transcend culture and time. Myths, or stories about archetypes often become part of folklore and mythology. These legendary stories about heroes are keys to, or blueprints of, how we can become more enlightened, successful, creative, or happy. Archetypes hold the stories of our primordial desires and fears and collective dreams. Jung writes,

> All the most powerful ideas in history go back to archetypes. This is particularly true of religious ideas, but the central concept of science, philosophy and ethics are no exception to this rule. In their present form they are variants of archetypal ideas, created by consciously applying and adapting these ideas to reality. For it is the function of consciousness not only to recognize and assimilate the external world through the gateway of the senses, but to translate into visible reality the world within us. [CW 8, par. 342] (Storr, 1983, p. 16)

Myth making has been the work of Shamans, medicine men, storytellers, and artists. As an art therapist, I work with people's symbols, myths and stories. We all play a part in creating and sustaining myths that reflect the guiding beliefs of our society. We can become more creative, active, and involved in our own personal and collective myth-making process.

The concept of archetypes can be traced back to the ancient Greeks. Carl Jung felt that archetypes function somewhat like instincts, by shaping our behaviour, and he believed that archetypes exist inside the human psyche. We see archetypal behaviour in ourselves, and others when we play the joker, teacher, mother, leader, and hero. Erich Neumann says that everyone must pass through "the same archetypal stages which determine the evolution of consciousness in the life of humanity" (Neumann, 1970, p. xvi). That is to say, "The self ... is the archetype of unity and totality" (Storr, 1983, p. 20). In seeking unity and wholeness of the self, we embark on an archetypal journey to find self-realization, or a Goddess/God state. In following the hero's / heroine's journey to fulfil one's highest potential – as on the road of the seeker, or the path of the heart, or following one's passion – the individual realizes his / her own self-meaning and manifests the inner spiritual urge or God/Goddess will. These poems come from the experience of working alongside women in these Artful Archetypal groups.

A POEM ABOUT THE ARCHETYPAL GROUP

I want to write a poem about my
Archetype groups. Something about how deep, rich, and
Mystical they are and how much I am fed.
By the groups of women who
Gather year after year to study with me.

I want to say it with simplicity,
Be perfectly plain,
So you would understand without my saying 'magical,'
Just how magical those nights are.
And without me saying 'sacred,'
Just how sacred those nights are.

I want to say it carefree, easy,
How we sit around the table and sew and paint
Our stories which, at first glance, may appear mundane,
But are now deeply significant and archetypal.

I never want to say
In hushed tones that I do readings at these groups,
Or whisper that part, because I am never sure who will judge
Or find that offensive.
But it is really very innocent and natural:
Something we all can do.
It's just reading symbols – ask Carl Jung.

I don't mean to go into all that
'New-age' stuff or deeply unconscious Jungian stuff.
I don't intend to get confessional
And tell you how
Every time we gather in candle light for our closing circle and readings,
That I want to cry.
It's so beautiful when women gather and share each other's
Deepest, darkest fears and support and honour each other as we do,
Because we all go through so much.

I don't mean to bother by telling that I don't really know
Why tarot readings work, but they do.

And I certainly wasn't going
To tell you the times I did readings
That changed clients' lives, or
Helped them avoid a serious mistake,
Or the times I had to tell unsuspecting wives that
Their husbands were cheating.

This was supposed to be a poem about how
Sacred, rich, and meaningful that the study of archetypes is
And how year after year I look forward to this group,
Because I learn so much every time I venture down this path.

I wasn't going to make excuses or justify
Doing readings. They just fit at the end of the night,
After a long, heavy heady talk about the archetype.
Sharing each personal experience
Through art and story
That we would ask the cards, "What does this archetype have to tell me?"
Or something simple like that.

I wasn't going to mention the word "Tarot,"
Or discuss why or how it works, or
The complexities of people's fear, understanding, or knowledge
Of something as simple as an ordinary deck of 78 cards.
That was never to appear in this poem at all
Because I never really talk about doing readings.
Yet, even as I write these words,
I can't help but think how natural it really is,
That someone asks a question:
"Is my daughter going be okay? Will I get the job?
Will things change?"
And the cards answer,
Somehow reflecting back the truth.

And I think about the change in atmosphere,
As we shift between the worlds,
Between the poem I meant to write and this, and
I want to say "why not?"
What is wrong with making room for this, too?

ARCHETYPAL DRAMA

My misconception is to act the Drama
As if I were alone, as if life

CHAPTER 10

Were something done to me,
But not with my permission.

To feel abandoned denies
The knowledge that I continue to pursue;
The knowledge that heals and questions.

My misconception is to act the Drama
As if my solo voice
Were not heard and could not speak
The thoughts of humanness that mattered.

My misconception is to act the Drama
As if my emotional knowing
Does not connect, attune, to help me move from isolation.

My misconception is to act the Drama
As if we all were not a bricolage,
Forming, changing as I write,
Revealing what is, suggesting what could be.
I don't know what wholeness looks like,
But I find glimpses in the faces and stories of my clients.
I have no misconception that tangled in these glimpses is wholeness.

CHANGING HOUSE

My body contains a group
Of confused, bewildered parts,
And thinks that the cure for emptiness is turning away from the others.
But knowing that somehow in the 'bumping up against,'
The 'rubbing shoulders of,' that something will happen
To fill that gaping hole.

In the hallways, The Wanderer paces back and forth,
Draped in her hippie robes and flowing skirts,
Poised to leave at a moment's notice.
Wanting to stay, but afraid that would mean,
Not being seen,
And she has perfected hoping that in the next place,
She will be different.

Down in basement lives the Inspired One
Cooking up her next plan,
Achieving stardom, knowing it's just a stairway away.
Dressed in fine leather boots and designer suits,
She is quick to laugh at herself,

But always wants more, this is never enough,
Fearing at the last minute, she will fail.

Deep under the covers is the Wounded Healer
Waiting for this to be over,
Knowing the pain will never stop,
And the gaping hole in her heart will never heal over.
Her nightgown, soft layers of white muslin,
Softens the fear that keeps pounding,
But not even the softest down feathers or satin sheets
Can make up for feeling it's too late.

In the kitchen, the Creative One is cooking up a storm,
Hoping to entice the others to visit.
Her graceful hair piled high on her head, faded blue jeans,
And flowered apron,
Dancing through the room, she arranges flowers,
Fills plates with herb-flavoured food, and
Writes inspirational notes next to each place setting.

Absorbed in a book, The Philosopher knows,
The answer has to be here somewhere.
Wrapping yet another beautiful scarf around her elegant neck,
Adjusting her dangling earrings,
She plays with the strands of beads round her wrist.
She trusts the process, but would like to know why.

The Seeker, holding court, talking, always talking,
Afraid she is talking too much, but can't stop talking.
She lives for moments of connecting, transcending,
And being, and works so hard to be, just to be.

The other women love her, want to help her
And often tell her she needs a holiday, or at least a hot bath.
Knowing she wouldn't even notice
Until she starts crying or is so tired that she can't fall asleep.
She worries about her hair – the length, the colour,
The just rightness or not –
As if it would somehow help her
Be more compassionate, less judgmental, forgiving, or wise.

The Creative One has finally got everyone's attention
And they all sit down to a meal.
As usual, The Wanderer has perched on the knee of The Seeker,
Wanting to be held.
The Inspired One talks about how

CHAPTER 10

The Creative One should do a workshop on
"Food, Mental Health and Archetypes"
And the Wounded Healer asks if she can take
A small bowl of food back to bed.
They all stop and look at her
Knowing that if they don't all pay attention to her,
None of them,
None of them will make it out of here alive.

THE FOOL ARCHETYPE

I am no stranger to this illusive archetype, having always loved newness, unknown edges, fresh beginnings and starting over.
Having always longed to hold what I can't quite grasp,
and being hopeful that I may reach my pure potential.
Believing that leaps of faith would have happy endings and spontaneous action would lead to happiness.
Often finding myself vacillating between chaos and order, wondering which way to fall.
Sometimes being naïve, playful, and other times open, fluid and free.
Knowing that living is an adventure and a chance to grow wings.
Understanding that seeing life through the eyes of wonder, awe, and simplicity could lead to realizing my wildest dreams.

I also know the dark side of this archetype, the dangers of leaping without a net, taking serendipitous turns down blind alleys, and trusting the wrong stranger.
I have opened gifts that trapped me, and followed what I thought was grace into dangerous dark corners.
And it is hard to hear the joy in Fool's laughter when it seems to be at my expense.

And yet, when I glimpse this archetype being played out on stage as the Court Jester, Bacchus, Dionysus, Trickster, Coyote, and many others,
I fall in love with her all over again.
The play, folly, risk and freedom that this dreamer and wanderer imbues in the world is so infectious that it restores my faith.
And after I catch my breath, I am ready to play again.

WE ALL HAVE THE RIGHT TO CAST SPELLS

It's the second night of the Archetype Group and I am teaching about the Magician.

He is the archetype that represents our ability to communicate to the world what our vision is, what we want to manifest and create with our magic wand. I explain that here, in the realm of the mystic poetic, the Magician holds the key to discovering our passion and uses it to help us discover our life work.
He represents our inner fire or creative energy.
I am talking about how he reflects our self-belief in our creative powers and abilities.
He is no dreamer like the Fool, he uses his charisma and charm to manifest greatness and grab centre stage.
When I pause to ask if there are any questions, one woman told a story about how she loved to sing in her grandmother's church choir. She would hold her head high and sing in a loud clear voice. And her grandmother disapproved of her boldness and reminded her that in the house of God, one kept their eyes down and head bowed. She wondered if from that day onward if her fire went out, if she lost the fledgling belief she had in her creative abilities, having no one in her life to fan the flames.

And the other women had similar stories of when they lost self confidence or had someone say no to their dreams and later developed fear of this archetype believing that it was for someone wiser, luckier or more beautiful.
In their lives, fire was something to rein in, control, not let get too big or bright.

And that night during the art making I wanted them all to feel that fresh spark of creativity when you paint the first stroke on a canvas, or start the first shaping from a solid lump of clay or write the first line of a poem and think, "Wow, I'm alive."
And maybe it is just a magic show filled with trickery and illusions, but hey what isn't?

THOSE WHO KNOW AND REMEMBER

All the archetypes hold pain and sorrow, how could they not.
But, the High Priestess' ancient suffering is the hardest of all to witness.
All the shadowy, dark injuries to women past and present fall in her lap
And keep us afraid of the dark.
She can't be bothered to correct the lies that are told about her chaos because words are not her medium and who believes a woman who speaks through intuition and silence?
And who cares about visitations, oracles, or sensitivity? These words are too elusive and full of shadows and cobwebs.
So, those who know and remember, sit and wait and dream of the moon and when Luna ruled.

So, those who know and remember, guard their knowledge of mysterious symbols and psychic visions.

So, those who know and remember, search for the gates of their own inner sanctuaries, when it is safe to do so.

So, those who know and remember, learn to witness and deepen their own silent knowing.

So, those who know and remember, learn to receive and commune with the spirits.

So, those who know and remember, stay silent but alert because they have perfected the art of waiting.

THE WORLD CARD

We are studying the last archetype on this journey, The World Card, the one that contains all the experiences of the past and hopes for the future.

And I am filled with Joy and Sorrow at this ending.

This archetype, representing our collective human experience that has allowed children to continue to starve, and rape to continue to happen, is also filled with the songs of birds and brilliant morning skies.

And we all have to make our way between the sufferings we have known and the sufferings we fear for our children's future,

And there is a reason for laughter and pleasure.

Even when we know about the deprivation, the slavery, and abuse that goes on everyday

We must have the grace to accept our gladness in the ruthless spinning of this world.

We must be able to turn the light around and not make injustice the focus of our attention.

We must admit there will be art and beauty despite the cruelty and pain.

And we are saying goodbye tonight, knowing that some of us will stay in touch and some of us will not.

And what we have created here, in this space together has added to the light that surrounds us when even we are doing harm to ourselves or others.

CHAPTER 11

ART THERAPY GROUPS AND CLAIMING YOUR RUBY RED SLIPPERS

These poems are from a group I created for women who wanted to explore change and transition. I used the *Wizard of Oz* as a metaphor for how change happens. Fairy tales, myths, and stories help sharpen our sight and present new ideas and instructions of how to move forward. In stories we can see the myths we live by, the new myths emerging, and the old myths being challenged. Clarissa Pinkola Estés writes that:

> Stories set the inner life into motion, and this is particularly important where the inner life is frightened, wedged, or cornered. Story ... shows us the way out, down, or up, and for our trouble, cuts for us fine wide doors in previously blank walls, openings that lead to the dreamland, that lead to love and learning, that lead us back to our own real lives as knowing wildish women. (1995, p. 20)

The *Wizard of Oz* follows the steps of the heroine's journey. The heroine's journey is a blueprint of how we as women move through change. In my art therapy group, we explore this in eight steps. The first step is risk: Dorothy leaves Kansas to risk the unknown. Our journey could start with the loss of a job, a marriage breakup, an illness, and/or a vague sense of discontentment. We realize things are changing. Dorothy's journey to individuation began when the one joy in her life was threatened: Miss Gulch was going to take Toto. Traditionally on the hero's journey, it is the male who goes out alone to face and kill the dragon, returning to the village a hero. Often, the heroine does not go out alone, but is accompanied by a young child(ren), an aging mother, or an entire family. Also, women's goals may differ from the hero's, extending beyond the personal to encompass the wellbeing of our children and community. And, unlike the hero, our journey may not be linear or logical. We may take breaks from our personal goals/growth to allow children to grow or husbands to develop careers. Often, we don't resume our journey until the children leave the nest. Now, we have to face the voices that tell us we are not young enough, not good enough, not strong enough, not smart enough, or not thin enough to set out on our journey. We must face and make peace with the voice of our inner critic, the voice of society, and the voice of our parents or partner that tell us we are not enough. This 'de-selfing' that women experience is the result of a society that does not always recognize female courage, intelligence, and emotions.

Glinda informs Dorothy that she's always had the power within to go home. Awakened, Dorothy sees that the shoes do fit; she truly can claim their power! What Dorothy now knows is that it was the journey and the faith and courage to stay on the road that mattered after all. Carl Rogers (1961) wrote that the "drive towards

CHAPTER 11

self-actualization ... may be hidden behind elaborate facades, but it is my belief that the need exists in every individual, and awaits only the proper conditions to be released and expressed" (p. 35). For Dorothy, the proper conditions appeared as she continued along the road to her journey's end. The poems *Ruby Red Slippers* and *Deconstructing the Yellow Brick Road* both describe different nights at the group. *Looking Behind the Curtain* talks about the different ways group members interpret and understand the material that is presented. The poems *Safe Journey* and *Group Art* talk about the group process.

LOOKING BEHIND THE CURTAIN

This is the night that we talk about facing the Wizard –
That person or illusion to whom we give our power:
The man behind the curtain.
We are making stages out of boxes, with curtains and dolls,
To show who in our life is the Great and Wonderful Wizard.

"I am Oz, the Great and Terrible. Who are you, and why do you seek me?"

When finished, we take turns talking about our art.
She explains how good they are for each other,
The curve of his cheekbone, his cologne.
She speaks powerfully of his knowledge, expertise.
Where she lives in a land of silence and darkness, he lives in full sun.

"I never grant favors without some return," said Oz.

How he can read her mind, know her thoughts before they're formed.
How theirs is a unique language, taught by him.
How she could not exist without him.
How she is eternally thankful that he is in her life.

"For they saw, standing in just the spot the screen had hidden, a little, old man, with a bald head, and a wrinkled face, who seemed to be as much surprised as they were."

And the group wonders how she never saw the wires hanging from the ceiling,
How she didn't know he was a ventriloquist.
There's an odd silence in the room as everyone looks nervously at me.

"Here are the other things used to deceive you. He showed the Scarecrow the dress and the mask he had worn when he seemed to be the lovely Lady; and the Tin Woodman saw that his terrible Beast was nothing but a lot of skins, sewn together, with slats to keep their sides out."

And I think how some journeys take longer.

ART THERAPY GROUPS AND CLAIMING YOUR RUBY RED SLIPPERS

RUBY RED SLIPPERS

In the group, "Claiming Your Ruby Red Slippers"
The last art experience is to create a pair of red slippers,
Full of symbols, ideas, feelings of empowerment,
Portraying inner strength and self-knowledge.

Anyway, that is the intent,
What happens depends on the needs and wants of the artist,
And the tone of the group, the phase of the moon, and maybe even how tired or not I am.
Those who run groups know what I mean, that line of tension that groups run on, sometimes magical and sometimes chaotic for whatever reason.
But what more reason do we need than there are eight women together processing their lives and doing art and sharing intimate details of their inner worlds?

Anyway, back to the shoes. My granddaughter walks around talking about *shozes* (as she pronounces it). She is almost two and she loves Grandma's high heels, boots, slippers and generally any and all *shozes*. What effect this will have on her in later life I do not know. But right now she believes that there are endless *shozes* in the world.

Usually the women in the group love this exercise. Who wouldn't? It combines symbols, art, fun, meaning and, of course *shozes*.

And some women in the group create elaborate mixed media installations showcasing their shoes, I remember one women creating a piece that lit up and the shoes spun around on a lazy Susan. Others used simple running shoes to work with because they planned to wear them after and really embody the artwork. And still others poured their heart and soul into creating a pair of shoes that could and maybe did transform their life.

And I am remembering all the groups I have facilitated and all the art materials I have collected; ribbons, yarn, silks and cottons, fabric paints, pastels, stamps, inks, endless amounts and kinds of papers, beads, buttons and the list goes on…

And I am amazed at the transformative power that can happen with a group of women reflecting on any concept, even shoes, and letting themselves dip into that endless flow of creativity that a table full of things can invite.

DECONSTRUCTING THE YELLOW BRICK ROAD

It is Tuesday night and our Art Therapy Group, "Claiming Your Ruby Red Slippers" is meeting.
Tonight, we are talking about the road.

CHAPTER 11

We all share stories about the scarecrows we have known and helped. Those helpless man who just needed someone to support them for a bit until they could stand on their own two feet.
And the tin men who needed us to mend their broken hearts at our expense,
And the cowardly lions, the men who acted tough, but were really broken little boys.
And of course, the Wizards, the all-powerful sociopaths that lied and schemed their way into our lives promising all and delivering nothing.
And the road, how it shined and glittered, but was really a setup for a naïve farm girl who was only trying to get herself and her dog home.
And if the road itself needed to be deconstructed and rebuilt so every woman walking it could get home safe or did the fault lay in the hands of Glinda leaving too soon, not helping enough?

LAYING DOWN IN THE FIELD OF POPPIES

That seductive resting spot, right before the finish line.
That feeling that we just can't make the last several meters,
Or hand in that final paper,
Or read that book one more time to our two year old child.
The lure of whatever calls us by name and the belief that just this once, can't hurt.
And the effort to takes to say no …
And the choice …
Always the choice …

SAFE JOURNEY

It is the first night of the Art Therapy Group, and we are talking about taking a journey together.
The art making centres around packing a bag, knowing what you need in life to travel down your road, what resources, what supports you will need, what nurtures you, all of that and more.
Some of the women make elaborate art pieces with sturdy backpacks holding the entire essential and nonessential things one could possibility want for a trip.
Others construct simple devices that hold the bare minimum, but would keep one safe and sound.
Others create beautiful nonfunctional pieces that look intriguing, but would not provide warmth, shelter, food, or protection.
And others having never travelled, or having never known what safety and support looked like, are lost, watching and borrow enough ideas from the others at the table so that they can pretend.

GROUP ART

You are afraid to do art, but you joined an Art Therapy Group anyway, thinking this would be better, hoping the therapy part would make it different, which I suppose it does.

And you are nervous, embarrassed that the others might make better art than you. So, you start telling stories about having lived in Russia and you spoke a few words of Russian, which made the story better. And you are safe, because no one else in the room speaks Russian.

And you keep looking at me like we had an appointment later, which much later we did, when you started coming every week to see me privately.

Then you sang a few lines of a Russian folk song, but stopped when you realized that everyone was still doing art and you weren't. But everyone was so pleased with your performance that they didn't want you to stop.

I reminded you that you don't have to do anything you don't want to do. But you started panicking, saying that you really did want to make something, and that the time got away from you.

And I said, trust the process.

CHAPTER 12

ART THERAPY GROUPS AND SOUL GARDEN

The following poems emerged from an art therapy group that I created called Soul Garden. I used the four seasons as a metaphor for how we travel through change in our life. Transitions between seasons are rarely smooth often we are on shifting ground. The ground we learn to sink into in the winter is solid, firm, and frozen, which gives way to the muddy, fluid soil of spring. Similarly, our moods fluctuate with the seasons: Life speeds up, new issues and concerns arise. We feel hopeful in spring; warm and content in summer; draw back with the autumn; and are often deeply inward during winter. In winter we tend to focus on internal issues as I talk about in the poem *Spirits* and in summer, external relationships. Constantly, we plant, weed, feed, nurture, and harvest our inner and outer life. Change can happen in a spiral fashion, moving ahead, while circling back as portrayed in *Prayer Flags*. Often, we feel we're covering the same old ground, dealing with the same weeds, but in reality, as we confront what seem like the same issues, we are seeing them in different situations and with different people. As we alternate between past, present, and future, we need to retrace some patterns, over and over. Spiralling inward to face dark, dreary winter days of doubt, eventually we spiral outward to glorious interludes filled with sunshine and warmth. Inner shifts translate into new outer growth. In learning to hold our ground, we create an environment conducive to growth as in the poem *Recognizing Life*, moving us forward through the seasons of our soul. This art therapy group provides a way to find our patterns of movement, change, and healing through the seasons.

RECOGNIZING LIFE

I remember the day when I felt I couldn't do this any more.
Grow flowers to cut and sell.
I had seen too much and felt too much to carry on like they were not aware of me.
It would have been simpler, to keep pretending that flowers did not have any feelings.
And I am not an innocent bystander here, I still buy bouquets and cut back weeds, fully aware that I am destroying life.
But, I could not stand being a frontline worker, showing up at markets with my jars full of freshly cut and slightly battered flowers looking pretty in their arrangements.
There are sacrifices for every choice, and even now, I struggle with the responsibility.

CHAPTER 12

PRAYER FLAGS

We are making prayer flags to hang in the gardens,
Sorting through the ragbag finding bits and pieces of materials,
Making stamps, painting, sewing on buttons, fringe,
Printing words and adding threads.
We are talking about Spring, the time of hope, new beginnings,
When seeds are planted.

Then one woman saw some cloth that reminded her of a blouse
She wore as a little girl.
And as we sat around the art table, drinking tea, sewing, laughing,
She began to talk about her childhood.

Most days, she said,
Father met me at the screen door
With a leather belt or bible,
While his hand reached under my blouse.
He said he liked his daughters clean.
He said I was coated
With lies, sins, lazy habits,
And God only
Knows what all else.

After – fixing me like a mannequin,
Tucking in my blouse, fluffing up my hair,
Adjusting my barrettes –
He reminded me that my life was hell,
In case for one minute I might think otherwise.

We all stopped talking,
But we kept on sewing. That is what we're here for:
To change rags into flags that could pray.

THE HEALING TOUCH OF NATURE

The healing touch of nature, tucked into the folds of the heart, like a Mary Oliver poem,
The things we forget; that walking bare foot on grass can heal, that staring at a blue sky can mend, and that feeling ocean water on the skin can calm what ever ails us.
That simple is sane.

SEEDS OF HOPE

Where I work,
Deep within mind, emotions, sensations,

Is a self, with a constructed reality;
A reality through feelings, beliefs, history.

Traumas experienced, decisions made,
Hearts broken, fears proven.

Where I sit, I reflect,
Listen, wonder.

In this belief system,
With these flooding feelings,

Where is the space? The place of rest?
The holding ground for sanity?

There – sensing an opening –
Is a place to pause,
A place to rest; peace to grow.

Planting dots of hope,
Maybes, and spaces

Of "could–be–different," gently,
In among the absolutes, the
"It-will-never–change" places.

Gently, so it can
Take root, grow, and not be
Yanked out for fear of being too
Hopeful.

Almost from here, I touch
My client's possibility of change.

SPIRITS

The talk has gotten off topic, sort of,
We were talking about turning inward in winter and the ways we had of doing that.
And somehow we ended up talking about spirits, and elders.

CHAPTER 12

And the three First Nation women in the group believe in the spirit world and know that our ancestors travel with us.

And the white women in the group, say nothing, for once, this is not their area of expertise.

I am talking about the teens that I work with from the valley who tell me stories about how haunted and cursed it is there, because of the legacy of the residential school experience.

And they say the elders tell them it will take seven generations to heal what the white men did to them.

They believe that the suicides, addiction, and mental disorders that the First Nation people experience, are part of the crisis of incompatible energies and the spirit realm trying to communicate to their people through these diseases.

They believe that the drinking and drugs that some of the people are trapped in, keeps them from aligning with medicines as prayer, sweats and smudging, so the powers of the spirits or ancestors can't get through.

And the white women in the group, not trained to understand the existence of the spirit world, having grown up on bible stories, are having a hard time believing this.

And I am thinking of when we, in the western world, hear a teenager talk about having spirits, or beings around them we drug them, never believing or thinking that these ancestors or spirits may be trying to help or communicate with them.

And I am thinking about many of the children I work with who have diagnoses of mental illness and it makes perfect sense to me, knowing them so well, that these children could be struggling with ancient ancestral energies or what we call generational trauma.

And I think that the way forward is not a severing of the past, or a belief in the future of genetic reconstructing, but somewhere in the middle, because try as we may we cannot pretend the past is still not with us and that ancestral spirits will not coming knocking.

But, as white people usually do, when we can't grasp the complexity of the situation, we want a fast fix, a medication that dulls it down and stops the irrational feelings.

And guidance from the other world, and voices from the ancestors, and rituals which heal are not rational or fast.

But, if we don't have balance between the relationships of the living and the dead, of white people and brown people, of family members torn apart by addiction and illness, then chaos will arrive.

So, yes, the ancestors who are not healed in the valley will continue to haunt the psyches of the sensitive and vulnerable teenagers looking for healing. And the larger cultural issues will stay stuck in the past until we all find common ground.

MOVING THROUGH THE SEASONS

The women are painting large beautiful murals on the walls of my studio showing how they move through the seasons,
Bright oranges, greens and yellow for spring and summer, more subdued colours for autumn and winter,
Broad strokes indicating living large and smaller brush marks showing quieter, more reflective movement,
Bringing in images, people, places, things that move with them,
Children, dogs, gardens.

I am painting also, images of my two year old granddaughter, running.
One day she saw me in my running gear, then later returning from a run, and decided that it must be fun, or maybe that was what legs where meant to do.
I am not sure how she makes her strong solid opinions, but she grabs me after work and says, "Karn, run."

So we run, back and forth down the sidewalk along my flower bed and we rest with our backs against the back of Studio B and I wait until she orders run again, over and over as two year olds are wont to do when they are shaping their world.
She sprints fast as her little legs will take her, the sidewalk like a race track,
Loving the game and running with wild abandon, as if nothing else mattered.
And later during the summer, on Denman Island, every night we run. Sometimes the track was the deck, or the deserted road beyond the cabin.
Breathing in the fresh island air, running.
And I love that for now, and maybe forever this is how she will move through the seasons, running with joy with her grandmother.

CHAPTER 13

ART THERAPY GROUPS AND DREAM WORK

Dreaming is necessary for psychic and physical health and is an essential part of the lived experience. Sigmund Freud discovered a basic truth about dreams - that they give a picture of the psyche as it is. Carl Jung took Freud's truth a step further, to prove that dreams also provide clues for future development. Freud believed that dreams showed us symbols that disguised and distorted the truth and were a secret code to be deciphered as in the poem *You Were Telling Me Your Nightmare*. Jung believed that dreams may be revelations of unconscious wisdom, but he also believed that the symbols and messages could be interpreted literally. Dreams signal moments in life when transformation occurs, preparing the dreamer for the next day or coming year, helping us to make wise choices.

Dreams speak to us symbolically. Symbolic language is a language in which inner experience, feelings, and thoughts are expressed as if they were sensory experiences or events in the outer world. There are two aspects of a symbol: the concrete (conscious) and the other reality (unconscious), and the symbol bridges the two. Symbols in dreams, religious tradition, and literature all share the quality of presenting insights into an unseen world (unconscious).

There are personal symbols, something that has become a symbol in one's personal experience as in *Home Room*; there are conventional symbols, such as a country's flag; and there are universal symbols, which emerge from the common experience of humankind. In art therapy I work with dreams through subjectivity, free association, personal amplification, and general amplification.

Working at the subjective level means that each part of the dream is perceived as part of the self. Free association refers to finding the hidden message by associating meaning with the symbol in the dream, as my client is trying to do in the poem *Recurring Dreams*. In personal amplification work, each symbol or aspect of the dream is amplified; consequently, spontaneous thoughts, feelings, sensations, intuitions, or memories are explored in response to the dream. In dream work, general amplification means that associations are made with mythology, history, folklore, anthropology, zoology, or any other branch of learning. The following poems are reflections on some dreams that I have had and some that my clients have shared with me.

RECURRING DREAMS

She slowly starts the session by saying,
"He always leaves me in the dream.

CHAPTER 13

He talks, but I can never hear what he says,
Because I am lost in the feeling of grief.
I call it my 'angst dream."

She talks as tears drop among the words.

"Is it going to really happen?
Is my unconscious mind warning my conscious mind of what is coming?
Is it guilt? Do I feel I don't desire him, so I torture myself with this dream?"
She talks as we sit and work out her feelings;
"Is it about my father and how he left my mother?
Is it my abandonment issues?
Every time I feel safe, will I have this dream?
Because, deep down, I don't trust anyone?"
She's making a clay bowl, shaping the sides, smoothing it,
Creating small designs along the top.

"Is it because I have a perverse need to torture myself?
Keep myself on high alert?
Or is it a release dream, releasing my fears as I sleep?"
She's adding small animals now dancing along the bottom of the bowl.
"What do you think?"
As she puts the finishing touch on the top of the bowl.

I think the bowl is beautiful:
So well crafted, so balanced.
She has a way of working with the clay.
It seems to like being in her hands.
There is a kindness there, a sense that she cares.
She has a natural talent. I tell her this.

She listens, then says,
"I mean the dream.
What do you think about the dream?"
And I say, "what more could I say that the bowl already hasn't?"

DREAM-WORK

One night I woke and I was begging you to stay in school.

I didn't have the right words and couldn't remember how to talk to you, that special language you and I use when I can really get you to listen and you nodding your head like you get it…
I remember the words came out cold and meaningless and your presence kept receding into the wallpaper in the bedroom.

And then I realized that it was just a dream and I was not really working. Falling back to sleep, I reminded myself that I had all night to get it right.

HOME ROOM

Room to grow.
Room to think.
Having no room for regret.
Making room for you.
There is no room left.
Taking up too much room.

Multiple rooms; complex, overlapping rooms; rooms with adjoining rooms: Making room for ourselves, our families, our place of work, our friends, our clients, our community, our world. How do we choose these homes full of rooms? I have had many houses full of rooms.

The farmhouse I grew up in had 11 rooms. In a reoccurring dream, I stand in a very richly decorated room filled with pillows, rich fabrics, ladders, paintings, and chests. There is the feeling of abundance, history, and wealth. I wander into bedrooms, rooms opening into other rooms, and the house appears endless. This dream usually appears before some form of expansion in my life, such as new work and/or new travel possibilities.

I call it my "abundance dream." The rooms are familiar, somehow, but at the same time, I see them for the first time. There are so many rooms, and they are filled with interesting objects. This dream always conjures up the feeling that I am coming *home*.
It has shaped me.
I don't know whether it comes to me or out of me.

But it calls me home.

YOU ARE TELLING ME YOUR NIGHTMARE

About teenage priests
On roller skates,
Bibles in hands,
Gliding to the
Rhythm of redemption.

Black flowing silk cloaks
On strong backs,
Now singing hymns
United in
Pride of righteousness.

CHAPTER 13

It feels like an old religion
That is now pinning you down,
Yelling at you about flesh and devil
In broiling shadows.

We paint it, talk about each character,
Look at the background, foreground,
Work with the imagery, metaphors, symbols.
Next session, you say the dream changed.

And this time you believe it.
Not a metaphor, you say, but a memory of a past life.
The nightmares stop.
Your best friend just took up rolling skating.

CHILDHOOD DREAM

Walking backward from the house,
Throwing stones, you run and run,
Stumbling into your present-day bedroom.

Closing the door
So you don't have to
Keep seeing that house.

You stare out the window,
But forget that you wanted out.

Lulled by the familiar noises,
You peer in for the thousandth time,
Hoping to see why
And how you ended up here.

YOU ARE DREAMING

You take out your notebook where you record your dreams
And start reading to me,
I, wanting something more real, fresh, try to get you to make eye contact, meet me here in this moment.
But you have different plans of how this will go.

And as you read, I find it hard to remember all the complicated plots, metaphors, and changing scenes as I follow you in and out of the dream series that seem to be going on forever.

You stop for some tea and explain to me that you believe that if you can take control in your dream world, then you will be able to control your waking life.

I ask you where you read that, or heard that, and I wonder out loud why you would not want to work the other way around, change your everyday waking life knowing that your dreams would shift.

And you look at me like I am mad, or crazy or have no right saying that I was a therapist who worked with dreams. And I feel like if I was wiser, I would be able to explain the backwardness of this, but right now, in this moment I am thinking, maybe this would work, why not?

And I have memories of backward days when I worked as a school therapist and the kids would come into my office with their clothes turned around and their hats on backwards.

And I am thinking maybe this could be a new therapy technique, or at least a tool for cognitive reframing, something like when a therapist would say 'turn that frown upside down' and believe that their depressed clients would find instant happiness.

DREAM CIRCLE

It's the night for our dream group to meet.
And we are going around the circle, each talking about a dream we want to work with.
And you are holding tight to a few words left over from last night, that will not leave you in peace but keep you on the edge of your seat believing if you could get the whole line, paragraph, your life would be complete.
Maybe if you paint it, you tell the others, the meaning will come back, be revealed.
And we all can feel that frustration when we wake with the vagueness of knowing more than when we fell asleep, but can't articulate why.

DUCK DREAMS

We are living in Calgary, and my partner is interviewing
The "duck lady" for the university paper.
This lady walks with a duck in her carpetbag,
Does psychic readings in restaurants.
Reading my fortune,
She says that later in life
I will be graceful, famous, and rich.

CHAPTER 13

I imagine myself – this beautiful, well-loved older woman –
Which triggers a memory of classrooms of snowmen
With beautiful round shapes,
That listen reverently to my teachings.
And, I am thinking,
The mind really doesn't know which is a fact and which is fiction.

CHAPTER 14

ART THERAPY GROUPS AND MINDFULNESS

The practice of mindfulness and art therapy are complementary paths on the journey of self-actualization. Practicing mindfulness meditation and creating art mindfully help guide us, calm the storm around our journey, and provide openings to access our inner strength and wisdom. The poems *Meditating* and *Just Sitting* talk about the practice of meditation.

In these two practices, one uses the breath, the other, the hand as anchors to guide and centre us. The one can complement the other or work in conjunction. Both practices help create the space within so that we can follow our spirit and passion. Both are "about discovering who we are as ordinary human beings. Being ordinary here means to start to recognize our true nature brilliant sanity" (Wegela, 1996, pp. 27–28). By discovering and becoming interested in who we really are, we become open, curious, and gentle. That is the brilliant sanity of which Wegela speaks.

Throughout our lives, we cultivate the habit of seeing things through the filter of our concepts and prejudices. Also, we have been continuously busy trying to distract ourselves from the pain and boredom of our daily lives as described in *Where's that book?* These dualities of judging and distracting keep us separated from the actuality of our lives—the treasure of the present moment (O'Neal, 1997, p. 8).

When we can fully engage with the reality of our lives in the present, we are practicing mindfulness. When clients in art therapy sessions are engaged emotionally, mentally, and intuitively in art making, they are being mindful. By using art as a tool to connect authentically with ourselves, we become available to the moment. "Art lies in the moment of encounter: we meet our truth and we meet ourselves; we meet ourselves and we meet our self-expression" (Cameron, 1992, p. 82). This centre or self that we meet can, through the practice of mindfulness or art therapy, provide stability and a calmness that is necessary to transform and heal pain.

Mindfulness blossoms when certain conditions are present. The mind is trained to be non-judging, patient, non-striving, accepting, and trustful. In doing art therapy, the same conditions of mind are cultivated. "Creation requires attention and complete focus. But most of all it demands that we take the plunge into new territory without knowing what will appear" (McNiff, 1998, p. 61).

To be non-judging, means to observe our thoughts and feelings without assessment. We simply watch, listen, and pay attention, without fear and without labelling what we are experiencing, as I explain in *It's Okay to Go in Circles*. We have greater freedom when we detach from reacting to feelings and move into accepting the feelings that pass through us. When clients become immersed in their art making, their desire to judge their work falls away. They move from perceiving their art as good, bad, beautiful, or ugly to seeing it as an indication of their present mood or feeling. They begin to see their artwork as process work—always changing, sometimes mysterious, and sometimes an authentic glimpse into the depths and beauty of self.

Learning one's own unique creative language and engaging in a dialogue with art becomes an interesting adventure. The safety of creating and seeing large feelings on paper helps clients practice detachment and gain distance from overwhelming feelings. Clients can paint their experience of one feeling state, then another, and yet another, and stay safely grounded in their sense of self while they witness and reflect on paper their changing emotions, feelings and thoughts. Rather than being swept away with these changes, the environment of the studio and the presence of the art therapist help contain the changing storm around the client. The poem *Witnessing* was written about this process.

Mindfulness also involves the vigilant practice of meditating on breathing and bringing our attention back to it when it wanders. Mindfulness means not becoming judgmental or discouraged when our thoughts race ahead into the future or continue to dwell on the past. The practice has us sit patiently until our mind settles to meet the moment. The same patience is needed as we stand in front of an easel or in front of a lump of clay. Mindfulness develops the patience to stay in a place of not knowing. "We enter into the confusion and mystery of whatever is happening with a curious, experimental attitude, not knowing what might be discovered, but welcoming, appreciating, and savoring whatever it is" (Johnson & Kurtz, 1991, p. 13).

For a client in an art therapy session to experience the ability to respond to whatever presents itself, the therapist needs to fully accept the client's experience of reality, quiet the storm around her/him, and help the client to ground their experience in clay, painting, or some other medium. The art therapist must be comfortable with not being in control, but be able to hold what emerges for the client. The therapist creates the safety and the containment for departure from known to unknown space; from entanglement to simply noting; from fear to acceptance.

The most powerful thing a therapist can do is to provide a setting, a nourishing womb in which lives can unfold. Through the physical setting and, most important, the setting of his/her own being, s/he creates a place of safety, a trustworthy place where all of life is befriended through an affirmation of faith in our wisdom and creativity (Johnson & Kurtz, 1999, p. 99).

The following poems come from my own and my clients' experiences from the art therapy and mindfulness courses I have taught.

BEING A BUDDHIST

Our family farm had big, wide-open spaces
For men, crops, and cows,

But it had no room for girls.
It had acres and acres of land,
But still we stumbled into dark corners
Where hired men lurked and locked doors behind.
Growing up, I learned to make myself so small
That I could fit into all my boyfriends' lives
Without them having to forget their last, or learn their next,
Girlfriend's name.

I blame my invisibility on my mother, of course,
Because of her craziness with not taking the comfortable chair,
With offering the last piece of pie to the guest,
And with bragging of having only two dresses.
I think that's why, when I became a Buddhist,
I confused letting go, with disappearing;
Acceptance, with dissociation;
And compassion, with letting people rob me;
Loving kindness, with giving self to anyone who asked;
Trust, with not having the right to ask;
Nonjudging, with not wanting;
And surrender, with rape.
It's easy to let go when you weren't ever there.

PURITY

I went to a Buddhist retreat last weekend
And came home depressed
Feeling that I am not kind enough, happy enough,
That I am too self absorbed, and self occupied.

And I dreamt that I had a baby, actually three
That I kept losing, and I was not really concerned or too interested,
That I kept stepping on the babies and misplacing them.

And I know that somehow this dream has a key or a message
That I cannot reach or understand.
But I feel calmer and comforted knowing that somewhere deep inside me,
Even though I keep loosing sight of it, stepping on it and misplacing it there is
a little bundle of purity, innocence and warmth.

I don't want to write another poem about loss, or grief, or not knowing
I stand too often in that blank space before hope opens up.
Instead tonight I want to celebrate not breaking open, having to bleed and
Laugh at the rubble.

CHAPTER 14

IT'S OKAY TO GO IN CIRCLES

It's okay to be angry. Anger wears itself out. It will end.
It's okay to be sad. Sadness finds its bottom. It will end.
It's okay to be tired. Tiredness finally nods off. It will end.
It's okay to be overjoyed. Joy drifts away. It will end.
It's okay to be hopeful. Hope becomes forgotten. It will end.
It's okay to be compassionate. Compassion will turn into worry. It will end.
It's okay to be angry. Anger wears itself out. It will end.

IN-BETWEEN

Holding on afraid to move forward or back like when a client clings to the door knob and spills out their pain at the end of a session in the in between place of not being in and not going out.

Or like when I am driving with one of the teenagers that I work with and they tell me their deepest darkest secret just before they jump out at their stop.

Or when the client that I do telephone therapy with throws out her biggest issue just as I say our time is drawing to a close.

Or when I am sitting in meditation waiting for the bell and all of a sudden, just then before the bell rings, I drop into the deepest, most expansive state of awareness.

Or like now when I am writing a poem and I am almost attaining what it is that I want to say and I realize that anything more would be too much.

WITNESSING

Working with others, I witness the walls,
the places where we become solid and sure.
A border at the edge of our willingness.
Sometimes wanting more, wondering what if,
We dangle a foot over the edge.
Watchful, but curious.
Playing with the unknown.
A meditation in form and formlessness.
And I witness the constant coming back to the beginning, a bit lighter for having widened the gap.

MEDITATING

Breathe in, breathe out.
Breathe in, breathe out.

A thought.
A thought.
A feeling.

Watching myself and coming back.
Breathe in, breathe out.
Breathe in, breathe out.
A thought.
A thought.
A feeling.

An ache in my back and coming back.
Breathe in, breathe out.
Breathe in, breathe out.
A thought.
A thought.
A feeling.

A deeper feeling.
Being watchful and coming back
To the breath.
Breathe in, breathe out.
Breathe in, breathe out.
Breathe in, breathe out.
Breathe in, breathe out.
Breathe in, breathe out.
Breathe in, breathe out.
Silence.
Silence.
Deep, still silence. Peace.

A thought.
A thought.
A tickle on my arm.
Coming back to the breath.
Breathe in, breathe out.
Breathe in, breathe out.

JUST SITTING

My teacher Russell calls our meditation practice 'just sitting'.
not expecting anything,
not striving for any results.
He teaches us how to achieve the right posture on the pillow,
how to achieve an open present mindful attitude.

CHAPTER 14

I remember when we lived on Pender Island
and Patrick and I made beautiful sitting areas all through the gardens, but we never had time to sit,
too busy weeding, planting,
playing with children.

Now, in the morning we take our coffee into the living the room
and sit before we meditate,
go running,
or look at emails
and we call it doing "old folks".
We just sit.

In the work I do,
there is a lot of sitting.
Sitting across from,
sitting with,
sitting along side.
Sitting with silence,
pain, fear and joy.
Sitting with whatever needs sitting with.

And I remember one of my first clients
and how at home she felt in the big comfy blue chair
that she sat in during sessions
and when I had her envision,
even years later,
her safe place, it would always be sitting in that chair.

The art of sitting.
Sitting with life,
sitting with all that is
and into all that we are becoming.

"WHERE'S THAT BOOK?"

By mistake, I left out an art book in my Art Therapy Studio that had pictures of naked women on the cover. In the world of art, this is understandable. In the world of art therapy with cognitively impaired teenage boys who live in group homes, this is disastrous.

Evan found it and excused himself to the bathroom for 15 minutes. In an hour long therapy session, fifteen minutes is eternity. In his following sessions Evan would repeatedly ask, "Where's that book? Where's that book?" and when I would innocently say, "Evan, what book?" He would say, "Never mind, never mind." Then two minutes later he would say, "Where's that book?"

And then knowing that he was not supposed to be asking say, "Never mind, never mind."

I am at a weeklong meditation retreat and my busy mind, as I am trying to be present, keeps thinking about Evan looking for "that book".

My mind is having nothing to do with settling, concentrating on my breath, or being present. And when the part of me that is patiently waiting for it to settle asks it what it is doing, it answers, "Never mind, never mind."

DOES HE HAVE YOUR BACK?

Why are you going to California again?, asks my sixteen year old client with a scowl on his face.
Because I go twice a year to see my teacher Russell, you know that, I tell him.
To do that stupid meditation stuff that you tried to get me to do? He asks.
Yes, we do that but he also helps me with my life.
You mean like a therapist?
No, different. He helps me wake up, be present and move out of suffering.
He looks confused.
He has my back I say, thinking he will understand.
Like you have mine? Yeah, I say.
Is he as tough as you are?
Tougher, I say.
I like him then. You can go, he says.
Thank you I say, feeling blessed.

GRACE

In my practice, there are moments of grace.

When Emily thanked me for believing her that the bugs were talking to her, because that's when she started to believe that maybe she was not crazy.

When Brenda told me that I was like family, good family, because that was when she started believing she deserved one.

When David's mother told me that his teacher could tell what morning of the week he went to art therapy because the rest of the day he would day-dream and sketch out plans of things that he wanted to invent.

Little pockets of grace, which when strung together help me make sense of the senselessness.

CHAPTER 15

ART THERAPY GROUPS AND A PLACE LIKE HOME

These poems explore how home affects my clients' sense of identity and belonging. Home can be described from multiple perspectives; however, home is most simplistically defined as something – a person or place – that creates a sense of safety and well-being for a person. There is a sense of belonging that may be experienced through body sensations of "being": centred, relaxed, free, nurtured, and empowered. It is an environment where roots can be put down, as in building a "home" make long-term plans; and envision living there into the future. Images of home are images that make us feel connected and safe in a place.

On a day-to-day basis, we collect, store, and remember images that create certain psychological and emotional states. This storehouse of images helps define who we think ourselves to be. These images are stored in the body as sensations; in the emotions as states; and in the mind as memories and narratives. Home often has cultural, societal, familial, and political connections, characterized by family and memories that translate into feelings of safety and love. When moving to a new place, one often feels in a state of abeyance, accompanied by ambivalence – excited about the new possibilities, yet alien in the new home. We live in this tension when we move to a new place. I have recently moved to Regina, Saskatchewan, and this tension has brought me to reflect on what home is for me. If my only real home is Self-in-Presence, is it necessary to feel 'at home' where one resides to be 'at home' in one's life experience?

We are builders, constructors of stories, images, and visions that bring us home and/or create a sense of home. I am at home, find home, and come home in my work. In my work as an art therapist, I help people find home again within themselves. As a trauma therapist, I have learned to wait for this process to unfold. When trauma hits, it has the tendency to scatter the pieces of one's life in many directions. Memories of the traumatic event become frozen and often replayed in the mind as a looping tape. The body can become stuck in 'flight-or-fight' mode and be constantly in high alert or numb. The emotions can either be repressed or intensified and, sometimes, both. Whatever the result, most people experience a disassociation or a sense of distancing from their body and life. My work is to hold the space for as long as it takes and create the conditions that allow the pieces of the person to come home. The following poems are from groups and clients experiences of talking and creating art around the subject of 'home.'

CHAPTER 15

JOURNEY HOME

My son always wanted to be in a cozy place. He liked to curl up, be held, maybe because he was conceived by a glowing fireplace.
He likes containment.

This is what I do in my work. I provide containment, a home for whatever is presented.

I fight against the domestic side of this word – "home," "house wife," "home maker." I am the maker of homes, but home where a feminist lives. I attended a faculty party when I first came to Regina and a woman, after learning I had moved to Regina, and my husband was already working at the university, said, "Oh, I just read an article about wives' who move to where their husband's jobs take them." All of a sudden, I was a wife, someone who follows. I am an artist, an art therapist, a teacher; I have never been a wife. That woman had just erased my career.

In therapy, I work with complexity and the invisible artifacts of power, internalized and externalized. Or is it really only decorating, rearranging what we 'see'?

At campsites, with flowers and scarves, I could always piece together a home. My friends say I create tableaus, beautiful areas, isolated vignettes. Is that doing therapy or doing life?

Therapists must search, analyze from different angles, and employ multiple therapeutic methods and interpretive strategies to examine different aspects of the psyche.

Is this not decorating?

When I teach art, I talk about having a central image, which Emily Carr calls a focus. In the piece, all the other elements should embellish, support, or help resolve it. The home in this project is the central image and the body, mind, emotions wrap around it. Our identity grows rich because of it; and through it, we come home to the self.

My daughter created Bunny World for my son and his friends. She and her friends dressed up, provided entertainment, food [which I had to make], and games. When my friend and her son visited Scotland her son [my son's friend] became homesick. She phoned us. He needed to speak to one of the bunnies from Bunny World to feel okay, to not feel homesick.

Home becomes embodied. The complexity of everyday life for my son and his friends became embodied in the reality of Bunny World.

When we moved here, we could not buy anything. Every time we ordered furniture, they lost our order or delivered the wrong item. We had to go to Calgary, to Ikea, to get what we wanted. Somehow, I felt slighted. At first, it was material for funny dinner stories. Then, I was promised jobs that somehow got lost or evaporated. I started to think that everyone here lied - The Land of Broken Promises.

Who or what is shaping my theories about my new home?

In Grade 4, probably my most disassociated year in school, I made a friend, rare for me, and started making and bringing her a gift each day. I enclosed the gifts in a paper bag. I still feel excited at the memory of her face as she opened the paper bag. I have often thought of having an art show where all the paintings were in paper bags and, to see them, people would have to open the bags and look inside. I would love to have the show in a schoolyard. Much in life had let me down by Grade 4, but creating these assemblages saved me. It brought me home.

Art is my home resource, my Bunny World, the place that comforts, makes well again my broken heart, my restlessness, and my angst.

I know that the making and giving of art in those paper bags has shaped me.

People keep asking me about the weather in Regina, as if it were a problem. It is extreme, exotic, it so real after continuous West Coast shades of grey. I love the rawness of it; I feel at home in it; it fits.

I remember being eight and coming home to my mother, who was angry and talking to my father. She never looked at me directly, but was asking him how a daughter of hers [talking about me] could do such a thing? It hurt me more than if she had talked to me directly and told me I was bad. I remember feeling happy at the time because things were good with my friends and also at school [I thought]. After I heard her talk, I remember thinking that it was impossible to get all the pieces to fit: Home, school, and friends. There was always a piece that did not fit.

How do we stay home with all the pain, suffering, joy, and desire of the human existence? I am 53 and I still can't make the pieces fit.

I am 20, have quit university, and returned home. This home is not a resource for me, but I have nowhere else to go. I am sick, wounded, and lost. No one in my family really talks to me or, if they do, I can't understand them. I sit for a long time. Then I start making candles. I saw an ad for beeswax in a magazine, and my mother must have bought it for me. I remember making 100s but, really, it couldn't have been that many. The making of candles, which now I view metaphorically, saved my life. It may have been why I became an art

CHAPTER 15

therapist. The making, the doing, healed me; it brought me home. Somehow, I returned from a very lost place. I started piecing my life together from scratch. I always seem to be rebuilding myself from whatever pieces are around, trying to make the pieces fit.

My image of 'home in Regina' is the sky. It's the biggest piece in my new landscape. Maybe that is why I came here: I am imagining myself home in the sky.

PRAIRIE PRAYER

When I told my friends we were selling our house in Victoria (Lotus Land) they said,"Why would you move to Regina? Are you crazy?"

They confessed their Prairie roots, having moved to Victoria from Saskatoon, Estevan, Regina, Moose Jaw, Earl Grey, and other foreign-to-me names.

"Did I understand the winters, the wind, and the isolation? What was I thinking?"

I listened, but romantic visions of Margaret Lawrence writing in a cabin, and paintings by the Group of Seven came-and-went to Joni Mitchell's "I Need a River to Skate Away On."

I joined an art group after I moved. We had a summer painting retreat in Bruno, in a wonderful old monastery. For 7 days we painted, and every day I ran. I ran in wide, open spaces bordered by wheat fields, sunflowers, and fields of flax just starting to emerge.

In Victoria I ran to the ocean. At Willow's Beach, I was grateful to be received by the ocean and all its moody, cloudy, sunny, and wild West Coast expressions. I told it about my day, how I felt, and what I was doing. The ocean was my confessional, my friend, therapist, and lover. It was home.

In Bruno I ran in the wide-open space between fields of wheat, sunflowers, farmhouses, and gentle rolling hills. Then, as the days progressed, it slowly changed. I wasn't running in-the-space-between anymore, I was running into the sky. I don't know how it happened: The sky just opened up and somehow received me, wrapped its arms around me, and brought me home.

NEW MACHINES FOR THE SAME OLD PRACTICE

Treadmill: *An exercise device consisting of a continuous moving belt on which a person can walk or jog while remaining in one place.*

While jogging on the treadmill at the gym,
Travelling while learning to stand your ground,
I wondered about roots.
Feeling far from the shaman's dance
And waiting in the underworld for my spirit animal's steps,
I wondered about memory.
Remembering that to travel lightly in a world,
Painless by our incurable desire to search,
I need to stand very still.

FOREVER TAKING LEAVE

So we live here, forever taking leave (Rainer Maria Rilke)

We raised our children in the wet, misty West Coast woods. When Willow was five, she knew the names of all the flora and fauna on the way up to Site Six. We built fences, studios, arbors, and memories. We worshiped in the stone circle, chanted in the tepee, and sipped tea in the garden. We called Willow our "bush baby" because she played hard and wild in her pink, lacy, fluffy dresses.

Can we attach to a house, to the land, in the same way as a caregiver? What if the feel, smell, touch, and memory of the house and the land can shape our future as deeply as a mother or parent?

We rebuilt the old farmhouse ourselves. Took the doors off, painted vivid colours on the walls, odd symbols, and strange images. We hung flowers and herbs from the kitchen ceiling to dry and made exotic furniture and clothes. Willow and Teiji created Bunny World, a world that happened up the hill at the back door. The house was a dream, an ongoing play, and an adventure.

Can home heal us, love us into being, understand? Can it patiently watch us grow up until we are ready to move out?

There were lots of little hidden areas in which to read, curl up, and dream. We had a stage in the garden for Patrick's Story Telling Festival, rooms full of books, and chairs scattered around the garden in which to curl up and read. A studio for me to paint in, play houses for the children, pastures for the animals, and a greenhouse for the plants. Rooms for doing, being, and dreaming.

When we left, we realized we would never put down roots like that again. Those roots went so far down they'd last us a lifetime. We were so nurtured by that land, that farm, the farm that gave birth to us. And, we have been blissfully homeless since.

CHAPTER 15

YOUR TIME

Because it is almost time for your session.
Because I am excited to see what you will make with this material.
Because you love sewing.
Because we get to play.
Because you are getting a bit happier and less home sick.
Because your body is calmer, and less tense.
Because all we get is an hour a week.
Because in this world, happiness has a schedule.

NOTHING IS IMPORTANT

Nothing is important anymore, he said.

Slipping deeper into the chair, the floor, the art work in front of him.

Away from the irritating boys in the group home, the concerned people, away from the reasons why he is stuck in a treatment program that isn't making him feel any better.

Away from the family up north that still loves him, but can't have him,

Away from this strange detour into foreign territory of therapy with others who have problems as big and small as his.

Away from his heart which may not endure this damage, the longing, the wanting to return home. Away from the pain of not knowing what will save him or his family.

Away from living in-between cultures, the one his Kohkom tries to teach him and the white culture which he keeps running up against.

Nothing is important anymore, he said.
"You are," I say.

BRAIN INJURY

The world does not make much sense to you.
You spend the winters pretty depressed but seem to wake up in the spring and want to do art, draw and write in your journal.
It's been three years since those girls beat you up in the park, the night you were drinking and someone, you can't remember dragged you home.

The hospital couldn't do much and four months later you climbed out the window in the middle of the night back to the same park where the girls were still waiting for you and the same thing happened, only this time your head injuries were worse and now you live in a group home and come here once a week for Art Therapy.

Sometimes you love being here and other times you look like you know that it's all a mistake and soon your brain will be functioning again like it did before someone took a metal bar to it.
But meanwhile here we are, painting, talking sometimes, occasionally drawing, but always waiting. You, waiting for the dizziness and confusion in your head to clear, me waiting for you to feel better, less disconnected, more peaceful. Like Art Therapy could be some kind of a pill that will kick in sooner or later and all will be well again and you will go home.

THREE YEARS OLD

She is only three and I am not sure that she really knows why she is here.
She likes coming, playing with all the toys.
I slowly start explaining that this is a place where she can talk about what bothers her, makes her mad or upsets her.
I say that even though we have fun, the reason she is coming is so that I can help her feel better, less angry.
She stops playing, looks hard at me, and then says, "Can you make my mother come home?"
And I say, "No, I can't do that."
She looks confused, and we go back to playing.

GRANDMA BROUGHT YOU FOR THERAPY

Your Grandma said that you needed therapy.
Your Grandma said, between tears and regret,
that what you have endured in your four short years of life was
more than anyone should ever have to experience in a lifetime.

And I am looking down at your thin arms,
acknowledging the chaos and anger in your eyes.
I know this job, this journey of mine is not for the faint-hearted,
And outside I hear the wind howling and the snow falling,
yet again, after it has snowed all week.

And I know that we will decide within seconds of meeting if this is going to work or not, this therapy that Grandma is talking about you needing.
You meet my eyes hard without blinking and ask me what toys I have and I know that a decision has been made.
And, for a while this will be home.

CHAPTER 15

SHORTCUTS

I remember an Art Therapist at a workshop saying that there are no short cuts through a bad childhood.

And that may be true, but I keep looking for comfortable places to sit and nooks and crannies that will hold us.

Small corners to call home, maybe not forever but just for now.

Places where when I lift another fear ridden narrative out of your painted picture, it will be strong and beautiful enough to hold the broken story that you tell.

And it will be filled with the words of healing and wholeness that you came to hear.

ASKING

Often, I have noticed that when reinvention seems impossible
And change too intimating
That the raw emotions that once appeared stiffly frozen, slowly melt into a little less vulnerable, little less edgy shape that feels uncomfortable but not alone, unfamiliar but not lost, and broken but not damaged.
Then the faint flickers of grace, presence, and freedom start bubbling up only because they were invited in the middle of a dark night to come home.

CHAPTER 16

ART THERAPY AND POWER OF TRANSFORMATION

After a cruel childhood, one must reinvent oneself. Then reimagine the world.
Mary Oliver (1995, p. 52)

This last section of poetry is about the art of reinvention. Art gives us the tools, the way to help reimagine the self and the world. The alchemical process of art helps us re-vision, re-create the energy that was once stuck in the body and psyche as traumatic and/or painful, into something fresh and new. The attitude of willingness to look freshly at old life material, take a creative risk and allow oneself to explore, enables an Art Therapist to facilitate her clients' journeys into finding her/his new unique voice, style, and way of travelling through the world.

When one is traumatized, deep in grief or depression, allowing even a little bit of flexibility, freedom, and fluidity into one's life, whether it is through painting, movement, singing, or dance helps shift the client into a more expansive right brain place which enables the client to begin to tolerate ambiguous circumstances, trust their instincts and engage in artistic revision.

I have often seen depressed clients start, with no enthusiasm or joy, to create something and then shift into a whole different mindset and body posture because they became engaged in an image that started to emerge in their painting or engrossed with the feel of clay in their hands. To create, one has to wake up to the moment, so you become present and awake. If a person enters my Art Therapy Studio dissociated, or disconnected, the action of creating helps reintegrate them to the present moment and for a while, they can become re-enchanted with life.

Art allows us to take scattered bits of stories and feelings and give them an expressive home. We learn to use images, fragments, sounds, and memories and form a mosaic, or map that points us in a new direction; not back into pain, but forward into the unknown. Art Therapy clients start to understand that the transformation of impressions and thoughts is a self healing alchemy that they can perform. We all do that performance differently. We learn to read ourselves and find what we need to heal. Our inspiration comes from our pain, our memories, our fears, and our anxieties and then undergoes a creative change in the artistic process to become our experiment, our design, or our pattern and then finally finds a home in a painting, a clay vessel, a song, or a dance.

When we rescue our memories and images from their isolated painful places in our bodies and minds, we reinvent ourselves. McNiff (2004) writes, "Welcome your chaos, your fears, and your resistance-they are signs that you are getting close; let the rhythm emerge from all of them. Stick with the process" (p. 236).

The creative process helps us understand that all parts of us are needed to create a whole being. We can't create from an illusion of ourselves or ignore the parts of ourselves that are difficult to work with or face. The blending, shifting, transforming energy knows where it needs to go. All you have to do is free it.

BROKEN IMAGES

You bring me your broken images

Which we decide can be reshaped into a heavy vessel worthy of holding all the pain and suffering.

But when we hold them individually up to the light, we start to notice the complexity in the patterns and the beauty in the cracks.

And we revisit the misconceptions we made in deciding what was sorrow.

And this pausing, looking again, gives space for old ghosts and sad stories to fly free.

So, we sink deeper into simple sights that we overlooked in our hurry to condemn.

The lost, the misunderstood, and fragile qualities we now see through eyes of teenagers falling in love.

And we decide to string them into necklaces and graceful bracelets, in despite of the flaws, and roughness of these now beautiful and precious broken images.

REVISION

I feel we are moving ahead,

I feel we are making progress.

You, no longer activated by the things that used to stop you dead in your tracks.

So much softer, kinder to yourself, no longer braced against the world.

Not letting painful memories cloud every new relationship.

And best of all, you let go of revisiting the past and dusting off the faces of your demons so that they could follow you around like some creepy eyes looking through the peep holes of eerie paintings in a cold dark castle.

And I know you get the urge to fuss around in those back rooms and check if you can still conjure up the feelings and thoughts that ruled you for so long.

But the fears really don't impress you anymore, now that you have seen how complex and satisfying the journey of going forward is.

And now that you know the ways of alchemy, the past is too small to hold you.

WHERE ARE YOU NOW?

We are sitting at my boyfriend's Aunts having tea.

And she is droning on about who knows what, I was a teenager at the time, and bored out of mind, sitting on a couch in a hot room, pulling down my mini skirt that kept crawling up my sweaty legs.

My boyfriend, his mother, father, brother and sister are all part of the picture, creating a circle around the living room table, sipping tea or eating dried out store bought cookies.

The aunt, tapping her cane against the floor to punctuate parts in her endless stories about neighbours, sister, or other people that I had no interest in, would every so often, stop her chatter and yell out the window, cane in hand tapping loudly on the glass,

"Where are you now?" to her small bent over husband dressed in grey trousers, white shirt and sweater vest even though it was 35 C degrees in the shade.

He, caught red handed, stopped short in his slow escape towards the road and out into the world, would creep back and reply, "Here, just trimming the hedge." And stare intently at the foliage as if his eyes could magically do the job of pruners.

And she, satisfied that he had not wandered off, would return to her story and I would sink painfully back into the couch.

And then a few minutes later, the drama would be repeated, him moving at a snails pace towards his great escape and her tapping on the window demanding his attention and obedience.

And now, my partner and I, taking conversations and memories as signposts and pointers, often say to each other "Where are you now?" as a reminder to wake up, be present in the moment.

And as an artist, I know that temptation to drift off, dream, wander, and search for greener pastures. But we all need to "live in" a world, one of our own creation or perhaps, as the old man, in one that is an extension of the world we perceive to be real.

Regardless of the making or maker of the world we live in, we need to be grounded in the reality of the here and now. So we ask each other, "Where are you now?" And we obediently, show up.

CHAPTER 16

BE HERE NOW

I worked in the school system with a counsellor who had given up years ago.

I did art therapy with seven children a day; he filed reports,

Hid on the phone, made cynical remarks at team meetings.

When last I saw him, he was going to volunteer in Africa,

"To make a difference."

Here, he felt, children's problems were their middle-class upbringing, their material wealth.

I tried to converse about making change where we are.

"If we can't make a change with the children we work with,

Can we really make change anywhere?

Who really needs change; the people we work with; or us therapists?

Who determines what the change should look like?"

You know, those conversation us middle-class white therapists can afford to have.

He wasn't listening, but I was, and after that day I decided to try harder at being where I was.

THE ARTISTIC MIND

The artistic mind in the flow,

Sees the world differently.

Call it what you will, synchronicity, serendipity,

There's a connection that happens.

It's an alert openness that receives what it thought it was looking for.

And of what it receives, it asks, what can I make of this?

MENDING A BROKEN HEART

She tells me that no one loves her, wants her. She is alone. This is after her home visit when she told everyone that she hated them and never wanted to see them again.

ART THERAPY AND POWER OF TRANSFORMATION

I am explaining to her that we are not separate from the rest. That we are all part of the whole. That feeling separate, cut off from others imprisons us, does not enlarge us.

And she looks at me like a caught animal trapped in her confusion of thinking that cutting herself off would bring her more, more safety, more happiness.

And she sits there feeling into the painful cracks in her heart where her mother, sister, friends used to live. Imperfectly of course, but at least better than the dark, cold tear that now rips down her chest.

And I tell her that nothing is permanent, we make this up as we go, cracks can be repaired. Mothers called, sisters texted, and friends talked to.

And I help her coax the small bruised pieces to unfold so we can mend, reshape. Just like when she comes and asks me to make amulets to keep the bad dreams out, and necklaces that will protect her from seeing her father and things to feel, touch when she needs to be calmed.

I tell her anything can be changed, altered. I remind her that she is an artist, and that is the job of artists, to make anew.

THE POWER OF PROJECTION

Apparently, we get what we believe, not what we wish for,

I say as she stares at the canvas not knowing what to paint, but pretty sure that it will involve pink paint.

Me, knowing how hard it is for her to talk when she comes here, thinking all she needs is an inkling, a whisper of a belief, say those words again.

She hears this time and lets it float around that interesting mind of hers, that I know collects things for the future.

The canvas in her hand, primed and ready for the background, starts leaning towards the tube of pink already accepting her images. I marvel at how good she is at this stuff, and I say it again.

EVERYDAY MAGIC

You phoned me, years after we had worked together

Now, I am not your therapist, but a friend who you call once in awhile to check in,

But this call was different, an urgency in your voice, a problem, your daughter.

She was different from your other babies

CHAPTER 16

Fussier, harder to calm, cried longer, harder when she got going.

Then you started noticing that she hated clothes, would bang her head, walked on her tiptoes, what did I think?

Did I think you should be concerned? Take her for tests? And we all know where this poem is going, but not quite yet, and not quite now.

Now, in this moment, is the time for something else. And I am not your therapist, I am not really your friend, but I fall somewhere in the cloudy area of mentor.

And I could hear Kate Bush singing her song, Circle of Fire, where she summons angels to surround her with Gabriel at the front, and I remembered a line in a book that I read somewhere about "standing on the battlefield, holding hands with the lord."

And I felt that emergency that all mothers feel when children's temperatures go up not down, and teenagers do not come home at night.

And we are on the phone so I can't hold you in my arms, but I can say that it will all work out, be alright, that this too will pass, that you will get through this. I can't remember what I said, but I can remember how it felt. Two mothers holding hands on the battlefield surrounded by angels.

CLICHÉS

You have come to pick up your daughter from her Art Therapy session, looking worn out, it's Friday.

You have been at a meeting with Sarah's social worker and caseworker and you are sick of hearing clichés:

"Everything happens for a reason"
"God only gives special kids to special people"
"We only get given what we can handle"

And you have attended all the workshops and talked to all the specialists. You are sick of fighting for money to cover your daughter's services.
And today, you are stressed, angry and don't know how or if you will make it through to dinner. So you sink into the couch, soak in the soft meditative music that I am playing, breathe in the lavender oil that is floating in the air and start playing in the soft sand tray in front of you.

And you are tired, a kind of tired that only parents with special needs children know, I say out loud, that I hope that doesn't sound cliché, but I think it does.

And we laugh. We laugh at the craziness of the moment, the world, my job, her life. And Sarah gets really excited and decides that she is going to be the Art Therapist. And she makes us both sit at the art table and draw and tells us to breathe deeply and praises our drawings and tells us how nice our colouring looks. And then she tells us it is time for McDonald's and I say that I never say that, and she says I always do and that she always gets a happy meal when she comes for her session.

So we go to the play kitchen and I make meals for us using the plastic food. And Sarah is happy, and you are relaxed and I am, cliché as it sounds grateful that I make a living doing this.

THE FOSTER SYSTEM

I asked my client last night what was the hardest part of being in the foster system and she said the lies. How she is never told the truth, and never believes that what she is told is the truth.

And I got an image of the tunnel of love, which was an old fair ride that I went on in my youth. You enter the tunnel and it is dark, but I remember it as scary and with things popping out at me and maybe that didn't happen, maybe it was a different ride, but I felt disconnected and weird on that ride and that is how I felt again when she explained that she kind of belonged in her foster home, but not really. She felt like at any time they could throw her out.

And you need to know that this isn't her first foster home. She has moved many times. It used to be her and her sisters and she was always the favourite, due to her ability to figure out what people wanted and how to be the good girl. She said it like it was a bad thing, and I told her that she was good at surviving. That it was a skill. And she thought about that and she said but because of it, she was lost. She said that she didn't know who she was. And I said, maybe or maybe that she had given herself a lot of choices of who she could be, and that she hadn't locked herself into one identity, she had lots.

And I remembered telling a friend that my mother had told everyone in my family what we would be when we grew up, except for me, and how much that hurt me. My older sister was to be teacher, which she became, my other sister a nurse, which she became and my brother a farmer, which of course he became. I felt, she thought that I was too dumb to "be" anything. Anyway, my friend said that maybe it had been a blessing because it allowed me to be what I wanted to be.

And that helped, my friend saying that. So I told the girl that I was sitting with, maybe having to be so many different expressions of herself will enable her to

CHAPTER 16

be her true self, having figured out who she is not. And she thought about that and kind of liked it.

Sort of like finding the backdoor into freedom.

WANTING OUT

The mother of these three children that we have all been working hard with has decided that she wants out.

After therapy, parenting classes, and group visits she said she is giving them up. Just like that. And I am sure it can't be "just like that", but I am talking to the Social Worker on the phone and I can't believe it. I see the mother sitting in a room telling them that she does not want them back and I can't understand how she will tell them.

The rest of the day I kept coming back to this, "How will she tell them?" Maybe it will happen like all the other chores that need to be looked after. Like sponging the counter, doing the laundry, folding shirts.

Maybe she will tell them she is too ill or has to go away. And they will go back to their new foster home where their foster mother will finish last night dishes and wipe away the crumbs from the afternoon snack before they all drove to where the meeting was.

And I wonder, some days, today in fact, how we keep doing this, water plants, make meals, change beds, wash floors when at the same time a mother, and don't get me wrong, I am sure her heart is broken, I don't know her story, is telling her three beautiful children, whom I happen to work with, and I do know their stories, that she is giving them up.

These children who get stomachaches when Mom does not show up to her visits, who get angry when they miss her and have lived for three years now waiting for her, don't get to go home. And I don't have a fresh supply of wishes but I wish I could tell you a different story. I wish I could say that she couldn't do it, that she said instead that she loved them so much she would stop using and stay home and do whatever it took to get them back. That tomorrow she would wake up early and make them a special "welcome back home' breakfast with eggs and bacon and jam and toast.

But this is the story that finds me again and again. And I remember a line in a Mary Oliver poem about being given a box full of darkness and realizing that too was a gift. And I am looking for the gift in this and maybe it is that I am not leaving these kids, and I know that is not as good as hearing that from Mom, but maybe we don't always get to decide what the gift is. And maybe sweeping the floor, making the bed, staying where we are, and not giving up is the only gift in this sad poem.

CLOSING

For me, these poems express the joys of living and working when situated in 'creative process.' Therapy is process work and art therapy is being creative about how that process happens. My hope is that these poems express change – whether a life change, a change in habitual thinking, or an emotional or spiritual change. In therapy, I help my clients explore where they have been, what that means, and where they are going emotionally, physically, mentally, and spiritually. We do this by staying present and centred in the creative process. This means focusing on memories, present hurts, and obstacles, and where they are felt in their body, what they look like on paper, the colours and textures that represent them, and the meaning they make of them. By slowing down and witnessing the substance of their lived experience, they see the behaviours or reactions they are experiencing because of the choices they have made. The key to change and growth lies in being present to the process of understanding what they are creating right now, through their words, beliefs, images, movements and feelings.

I hope these poems reflect the flexible, divergent, original, free, and fluid work of therapy. When we are grounded in creativity, we move in a healthy, holistic way to experience the insights, new ideas or feelings that we are wanting. My hope is that these poems ask 'what if?' challenge, and engage in artistic improvisation.

COLOUR BLIND

I asked my daughter to read my poems
wanting her approval,
And she wanted to know why I didn't talk about all the successful clients.
The good work I do.
Why were they so sad, so dark?
And I was confused because I thought,
I was writing about the successes,
the good work
and that the poems spoke of hope.
But most of all,
I wanted to her to understand the darkness.
Explain to her that we all to have to embrace it,
make a bed of peace in it.
That life was not only all about living in,
and searching for the light.
That my clients were wise and kind,
because of their lessons of defeat, suffering,
and deep grief.

CLOSING

And success was not finding your way out of the depths,
But learning how to accept and be with your darkness,
that acceptance transforms the hold it has on us.
And that standing in the darkness without
Any trace of fear, clinging, or surrender
Makes my clients have an appreciation, an understanding of life
That fills them with compassion, gentleness
And a deep love for the light, which is really only the flip side,
can't have one without the other.
And then I started thinking,
and perhaps as with so much else
between my daughter and me,
it's not about dark or light at all,
but getting lost in the mutable shades of grey.

REFERENCES

Cameron, J. (2002). *The artist's way: A spiritual path to higher creativity.* New York, NY: J.P. Tarcher/Putnam.

Estés, C. P. (1995). *Women who run with the wolves: Myths and stories of the wild woman archetype.* New York, NY: Random House Press.

Johnson, G., & Kurtz, R. (1991). *Grace unfolding psychotherapy in the spirit of the tao-te ching.* New York, NY: Bell Tower.

McNiff, S. (1998). *Trust the process.* Boston, MA: Shambhala Press.

McNiff, S. (2004). *Art heals: How creativity cures the soul.* Boston, MA: Shambhala Press.

Neumann, E. (1970). *The great mother: An analysis of the archetype.* Princeton, NJ: Princeton University Press.

Oliver, M. (1995). *Blue pastures.* New York, NY: Mariner Books.

O'Neal, J. S. (1997). Mindfulness: Treasuring the moments. *Creative Nursing, 3*(3), 8–10.

Rilke, R. M. (1980). *Eighth Duino Elegy. The selected poetry of Rainer Maria Rilke.* S. Mitchell (Trans.). London, UK: Picador.

Rogers, C. (1961). *On becoming a person: A therapist's view of psychotherapy.* New York, NY: Houghton Mifflin.

Storr, A. (1983). *The essential Jung.* Princeton, NJ: Princeton University Press.

Wegela, K. K. (1996). *How to be a help instead of a nuisance: Practical approaches to giving support, service, and encouragement to others.* Boston, MA: Shambhala Press.

Printed in the United States
By Bookmasters